COMPANIES BUILT TO LAST

FRANS DE GROOT

A PROVEN METHOD FOR SUSTAINING BUSINESS SUCCESS

BISPUBLISHERS

Copy editing by John Holloway
Design by Lilian van Dongen Torman

BIS Publishers
Timorplein 46
1094 CC Amsterdam
The Netherlands
bis@bispublishers.com
bispublishers.com

ISBN 978 90 636 9951 2

TO AMBER & BAS

SUCCESS ISN'T ROCKET SCIENCE - IT'S ABOUT KNOWING THE RIGHT INGREDIENTS.

AND GUESS WHAT? I'M HERE TO SHARE THE RECIPE WITH YOU!

Preface

This book you're holding introduces the Bitsing method, a revolutionary approach to strategy, operations, and financial management that delivers guaranteed results. Developed through years of hands-on experience and validated by real-world case studies, this scientifically proven method is built on seven essential principles—each one reinforcing the next to create a powerful, results-driven framework.

The application of Bitsing by so many organisations and individuals, in every corner of the world, has helped us all perfect and master the practical application of the method, and has helped me convey it to people in numerous inspiration sessions over the years.

I felt it was time to set out the ultimate result of all of our Bitsing efforts in a practical 'how to' book. A comprehensive, clear guide for the practical application of this proven method for sustained business success. A handy guide for everyone who aims to achieve their goals with Bitsing. Hence the fitting title: *Companies Built to Last*.

This book is for anyone who's in the trenches, fighting for growth and longevity. It's also for the dreamers and the doers who are aiming for the stars – aiming to build a company that stands the test of time. From global brands to startups, from multinationals to solo entrepreneurs, from managers to frontline workers, from seasoned professionals to eager students, from business owners to CEOs – everyone can benefit from the insights of the inspiring Bitsing method.

INTRODUCTION	9
THE SECRET OF BITSING	11
CONTINUITY AND GROWTH TEST	20
STEP 1: WITHOUT A GOAL, YOU ACHIEVE NOTHING	28
STEP 2: GUARANTEE YOUR SUCCESS BY FOCUSSING ON HARD FINANCIAL FACTS	46
STEP 3: YOU ARE UNBEATABLE	74
STEP 4: MAKE THE MOST OF EVERY PERSON IN YOUR TARGET GROUP	100
STEP 5: THIS IS HOW YOU DEPLOY EFFECTIVE PROCESSES AND PROGRAMMES	134
STEP 6: PREDICT YOUR RESULTS BEFORE ROLLING OUT YOUR PROGRAMMES	166
STEP 7: ENSURING PROFIT AND AVOIDING FINANCIAL DISASTERS	194
GLOSSARY	210
BITSING CHECKLIST	216
CLOSING REMARKS & A WISH	219
A THANK YOU	220

Introduction

Every organisation, from small businesses to large corporations, faces the daily challenge of ensuring its continued existence. Whether they have just one or tens of thousands of employees, organisations continuously strive to answer the most crucial question, 'What does it take to be successful?' And, in turn, what goals should we set? Which direction should we take? How should we position ourselves in the market? What exactly should we do? What resources can we allocate to achieve this? As well as many other, critical questions.

But what are the real answers? The truth is, we don't know. We're all fumbling in the dark, relying on gut feel and past experience. Spoiler alert: yesterday's tricks might not cut it tomorrow.

So what do we do? We dive into complex theories and fancy jargon, trying to convince ourselves (and others) we're on the right track. Sounds familiar? Let's face it, for most organisations the results are as disappointing as a flat tire on race day. Thousands of businesses crash and burn, and the main reason is that we simply don't know enough about what makes a company continue to tick in the long haul.

So, hang onto your hat! I'm about to take you on a wild ride through the most mind-blowing management method of our time. The Bitsing method is the world's first and only method that actually tells you what you need to know to build a company that lasts. It isn't just theoretical - it's been rigorously tested in academic settings and proven effective in the daily operations of numerous organisations in a variety of industries.

I'm not going to bore you with theory. Nope, we're diving straight into the nitty-gritty – how to use this method in your day-to-day business life. How to make it work for you. Each chapter contains real-world examples that will bring you back down to earth, show you the simplicity and logic behind the method, and demonstrate how to achieve your goals using common sense. Think of it as your personal coach, guide and cheerleader – all rolled into one!

Once you start reading, you won't be able to put this book down. When you see the logical, easy-to-understand models, you'll want to apply them right away. And guess what? You can! I've made every effort to write everything in clear, accessible language. No frills, no lengthy theoretical discourses.

With Bitsing, that's simply not necessary. Bitsing will take you straight to the decisions you have to make and how to make them in order to make your company, institution or organisation successful. Ready to build a company that lasts? Let's go!

The Secret of Bitsing

It's extraordinary that the place where the world's first multinational was founded in 1602, where the world's first share was issued and where the first stock exchange was established, is also the birthplace of the first method that guarantees spectacular increases in the value of any share and every organisation. Yes, the Bitsing method was discovered in Amsterdam, the Netherlands.

Before I explain how to implement Bitsing, let me first take you through its history. It's an incredible story, in itself.

The Origins of A Revolutionary Model

To trace the origins of Bitsing we must journey back three decades to the early 1990s, when I founded my marketing communications agency, KMM Amsterdam. This agency was unique in its approach and so successful that by its third year one of the largest, global advertising agencies (Lintas Worldwide, with 160 offices across 50 countries) sought to acquire it. At the time I hadn't yet realised that the Bitsing method was the foundation of my agency's success.

My journey to this point had been colourful, spanning years in marketing followed by leadership roles in international marketing communication agencies. In this period I not only garnered numerous international awards but, more importantly, a wealth of knowledge and experience.

Alongside my primary career, I ventured into entrepreneur-ship, experiencing the highs and lows that come with building businesses. They taught me first-hand what it means to achieve goals and succeed as an entrepreneur. During my marketing career, I invented and marketed a unique product which, with minimal investment, achieved sales of millions of units. This success kept an Italian factory operating 24/7 and ultimately led to the sale of the business to one of Europe's largest home products retailers. This venture, undertaken in addition to my regular work, exemplifies the potential for success when you pursue a truly unique and uncopyable idea.

I share this story to illustrate a crucial point: when your business is genuinely unique and impossible to copy, success naturally gravitates towards you.

The phenomenal success of both my home product concept and my marketing communications agency stemmed from their unbeatable nature. In chapter 3 I'll guide you through the process of making your organisation equally unbeatable, using the Bitsing method – which encapsulates everything I've learned and experienced over the years.

An Extraordinary Discovery

Returning to the early days of KMM Amsterdam in the '90s, we quickly attracted a prestigious clientele, including several British car brands, then belonging to the BMW group. These brands were facing declining sales despite extensive marketing efforts. I won their business with an unconventional approach to markets and target groups.

The plan I developed for them was based on six steps. Unknown to anyone at the time, this approach was the embryonic form of what would become the Bitsing method. The implementation of the plan resulted in something extraordinary: sales of the relevant cars doubled – achieving a 200% growth rate. One of the car brands became the fastest-growing brand in Europe, a feat unprecedented in its history! How was this 'impossible' growth achieved?

The secret behind this remarkable success remained elusive, even to me. The only clue lay in the 6-step plan, which would prove pivotal in the years to come. This template was subsequently used to develop marketing and communication plans for other clients, such as Sony, WWF, British Airways,

Philips, and many more. All consistently yielding results that far exceeded expectations.

The revelation of the secret behind these successes came later, in a moment that felt like a scene from a film. One day, while reviewing the table of contents of my highly successful BMW Group Brands plan, I noticed something extraordinary.

The first letter of each chapter title, representing the six steps of the plan, spelled out a word 'BITSER'. And this plan amounted to a model prescribing six distinct activities which, when applied to a market, target group or individual, delivered unprecedented results.

This BITSER model is now recognized as the original or basic Bitsing model, forming the foundation of the entire management method. Chapter 4 of this book provides a detailed guide on how to use the model. However, to grasp Bitsing as a method, one must first understand the original 'basic Bitsing model'. This will quickly convince you of its capacity to optimise everything you and your organisation do.

The Basic Bitsing model

The six letters of BITSER each hold a key to success. Before delving into what these letters stand for and how to use the method, let's uncover the secret behind them.

True success in approaching markets and target groups is achieved only when every individual in these groups does what you want them to do. Every single one! If only a small group responds to your organisation, its activities, and messages, you will have missed the majority and achieved very little.

Consider this: out of the hundreds, thousands, or even tens of thousands in your most important target group, how many people actually do what you ask? Whether it's buying your product or service, changing their behaviour or visiting your premises, it's always a limited number that do exactly what you want. Always a small minority. The reason? You've probably only applied one, or some, of the six aspects of the BITSER model, and not all six. You're not doing it wrong; you're just not doing enough.

NOBODY IS, THINKS, OR ACTS THE SAME!

If you require a target group to all do the same thing (for instance to buy, in response to a sales message), you may only affect a few individuals and certainly not everyone. People are unique and think and act differently. Focusing purely on sales, marketing, having the perfect product or providing customer services is, on its own, insufficient. Real success comes from the correct *mix* of activities, focused on ethical correct groups of people, at the correct time and the BITSER model tells you exactly how to determine that mix. Amazingly, there are only six activities in this mix.

A Six-Step Stairway

Although the concept of a 'funnel' is now common in many organisations, I may have discovered the first 'funnel' in the early nineties. The BITSER model is indeed simple – a stairway with six steps. Every individual in a target group will climb these six steps, and when they reach the top, they will have satisfied your objectives. If they don't reach the top, it's because you haven't been successful in helping them to climb. This is often because you've done the wrong thing, or done too little, or nothing at all.

Everyone in your organisation, whether it's a multinational or a one-person business, is there for the same reason – to help the people in your target group climb the Bitser stairway and achieve the organisation's objectives. Even those employees who are not directly in contact with the market or target group play a vital role in this process.

It's time to discover what the first letters of the six chapter titles of that significant BMW Brands plan represent. This is where the stairway and the six steps of the BITSER model first took form. We'll start with the first chapter. This is the first step, at the bottom of the BITSER stairway, where everyone in your target group starts:

B

Brand awareness
The first chapter of the BMW Group Brands plan started with a 'B'. It was entitled 'Brand awareness'. It's the foundation, where everything starts. If no one knows your name, you can't expect to be recognised or to achieve your goals.

I

Image
The second chapter of the BMW Group Brands plan started with an 'I'. The 'I' stands for Image. This is attained when you move people from just having brand awareness, to wanting your brand. 'I want you' is a crucial requirement for progressing along the BITSER journey.

T

Traffic
The third chapter started with a 'T' - for 'Traffic in dealer showrooms'. 'T' is for Traffic. This step requires movement towards the purchase point, whether it's visiting a physical shop, a web shop or making a sales appointment.

	Sales
S	'S' was the first letter of chapter four of my BMW plan – 'Sales promotion'. This chapter was about achieving Sales. It could be the sale of a product or service, but also achieving a new employee's signature on an employment contract, or any act by a person who is doing what you want them to do.

	Extra Sales
E	The title of the fifth chapter started with an 'E', for 'Extra sales'. This step involves repeat purchases, upselling, or – in a motivation or training programme, for instance – continued performance of desired conduct by employees.

	Referral Sales
R	The title of the sixth chapter started with an 'R' - for Referral sales. It's the final step of the BITSER model, in which existing clients become ambassadors, selling your product, service or goal to others, without your intervention.

You now understand the BITSER model - and you know where it comes from. The six steps of the BITSER model are timeless and universally applicable. They work for every organisation and objective. Every employee operates at the level of one or more of these steps, whether recruiting customers, achieving growth, recruiting staff, generating revenue and profit, improving employee performance, changing behaviour, or even recruiting votes for a political party.

From BITSER to Bitsing

In the years following the discovery of BITSER, many organisations applied it. With measurement, learning, optimisation,
numerous practical case studies and collaboration with colleges
and universities in various countries, the model continued to
improve and it became increasingly effective.

THE SUCCESS OF THIS APPROACH
SPARKED MY CURIOSITY AND SET
ME ON THE PATH OF DEVELOPING
WHAT WOULD BECOME THE
BITSING METHOD.

The BITSER model evolved into a comprehensive method
encompassing virtually all the factors that determine an
organisation's success. I called the method Bitsing.

The first four letters pay homage to the discovery of the first
four steps of the BITS stairway and are also a nod to the fact that
the method encompasses 'all the bits and pieces' – i.e. the entire
organisation, including its success factors. The 'ing' in Bitsing
indicates that ensuring an organisation's continuity and growth
is an ongoing process, a continuous action. Bitsing relates to
process, activities, and a continuous state of engagement with
all the bits and pieces of your organization.

For more than two decades, I tracked hundreds of companies,
organisations and individuals who had applied the BITSER model
and achieved their goals. I was able to examine their successes
and failures as revealed in the scientific research conducted in
the European university master's program, in collaboration with
four leading European universities.

This revealed that businesses and organizations had effortlessly achieved their goals, growing explosively, with some growing at precisely the magical rate of 300%!

Most importantly seven common elements emerged from these cases, which defined what we mean by a 'Company Built to Last'. These seven, revolutionary insights amount to a guaranteed success formula for creating a Company Built to Last. They make objectives achievable and assure continuity and growth in seven, quick, easy steps. These steps are referred to as the seven Bitsing principles:

1	They were all guided by a continuity objective (crucial for survival).
2	They guaranteed their success by focusing on hard, financial facts (and did not diverge from this).
3	Their approach to their markets was unbeatable, outclassing competition.
4	They had the ability to get everything they wanted from every member of their target groups.
5	They used effective programmes, both externally with customers and internally among employees.

6	They predicted the results before rolling out activities.
7	They invested less in their activities than they expected to earn from them, thus guaranteeing profitability.

I have now introduced you to the Bitsing method. In the next seven chapters, I'll clearly explain the Bitsing method and its models, in theory and in practice. I'll deal with each of the method's laws, one by one. And I'll put you in a position to use Bitsing to book unprecedented successes. You'll experience, for the first time, the real basis for the successful achievement of your goals, and how up-front prediction of results guarantees success and a positive financial return on your investment.

TODAY'S BITSING METHOD IS THE CULMINATION OF OVER 30 YEARS OF SCIENTIFIC RESEARCH AND PRACTICAL APPLICATION.

The Meaning of 'Continuity' in This Book

A study [1] by McKinsey & Co. found that the average life-span of companies listed in Standard & Poor's 500 was 61 years in 1958. Today, it is less than 18 years. McKinsey believes that, in 2027, 75% of the companies currently quoted on the S&P 500 will have disappeared.

Throughout this book, you will frequently encounter the word 'continuity'—but not in the conventional English sense of disaster recovery or restoring business operations after a crisis. In the Bitsing method, continuity is not about merely surviving; it is about thriving, progressing, and ensuring lasting success. It means building a company that is not just resilient in the face of challenges but one that continuously grows, evolves, and secures its future.

This book is not about avoiding calamity—it is about creating a business that is built to last.

Take the Bitsing Continuity and Growth Test

Let's assess how well your organization ensures its continuity and growth. This test is based on the scientific criteria of the Bitsing method. Choose one answer for each question. You'll get your results immediately after completing the test. But if you redo the test after reading the book, you'll notice a surprisingly higher score. Because you'll have a better understanding of what it takes to build an organisation that's built to last.

The correct answers can be found on page 25. Be honest when answering and don't peek ahead!

---

1 https://www.mckinsey.com/capabilities/mckinsey-digital/our-insights/building-new-businesses-how-incumbents-use-their-advantages-to-accelerate-growth

1

ANSWER 1   ANSWER 2

THE GOAL OF OUR ORGANIZATION IS:

A A social goal
B An environmental goal
C A financial goal
D A marketing/sales goal

2

ANSWER 1   ANSWER 2

GOAL-SETTING IN OUR ORGANIZATION IS:

A Individual (everyone has a personal goal)
B Collective (as a team)
C Non-existent
D Guided by market developments

3

ANSWER 1   ANSWER 2

OUR ORGANIZATION IS CURRENTLY FOCUSED ON:

A Innovation
B Reorganization
C Change
D Maintaining consistency

4

ANSWER 1   ANSWER 2

THE STRATEGIC FOCUS OF OUR ORGANIZATION IS PRIMARILY ON:

A People
B Financial resources
C Processes & systems
D Corporate Social Responsibility (CSR)

5

ANSWER 1   ANSWER 2

WE BASE OUR CHOICES MAINLY ON:

A Data from systems
B Gut feeling or intuition
C Current facts
D Experience

6

ANSWER 1 ANSWER 2

OUR ORGANIZATION'S STRATEGY IS PARTLY DETERMINED BY:

A Advice from reputable parties
B An integrated approach across all departments/business units
C Internal brainstorming sessions
D Business models

7

ANSWER 1 ANSWER 2

WE ARE:

A Exceptionally distinctive and unique
B Certainly the best
C Unrivalled
D Competitive

8

ANSWER 1 ANSWER 2

WHAT MAKES US SO SPECIAL IS MAINLY:

A Our brand
B Our product/service
C Our internal organization
D Our pricing

9

ANSWER 1 ANSWER 2

SUCCESS COMES TO US THROUGH:

A Who we are
B What we do
C The image others have of us
D Continuous improvement

10

ANSWER 1 ANSWER 2

OUR ACTIVITIES ARE FOCUSED ON:

A Acquiring new customers
B Retaining and creating loyalty among existing customers
C Creating an increased brand awareness
D A balanced mix dictated by market facts

11

ANSWER 1   ANSWER 2

WHICH OF THE FOLLOWING MOSTLY APPLIES TO US?

A   Each of us knows what the others are doing
B   Some departments are 'invisible'
C   All employees work together (can't do without each other)
D   There are departments that feel superior to others

12

ANSWER 1   ANSWER 2

WHEN WE APPROACH MARKETS AND TARGET GROUPS:

A   We use a shotgun approach
B   We let individuals in the target group take the initiative to contact us
C   We guide members of the target group individually towards our objectives
D   We focus on the customer journey

13

ANSWER 1   ANSWER 2

WE KNOW HOW TO EFFECTIVELY MANAGE OUR OPERATIONAL ACTIVITIES TO:

A   Prioritize
B   Organize
C   Plan
D   Monitor

14

ANSWER 1   ANSWER 2

OUR ORGANIZATION WORKS, AS A WHOLE, TO:

A   Achieve maximum results with minimum effort
B   Execute actions that help realize our goal
C   Conceive and create new concepts and objects
D   Realize as many sales as possible

15

ANSWER 1   ANSWER 2

WITH REGARD TO OUR SPECIFIC ACTIVITIES:

A   We do what we always do, but we do that well
B   We know exactly what we're doing
C   We know why we do what we do
D   We integrate a mix of essential activities

16

ANSWER 1   ANSWER 2

OUR POSITIVE PERFORMANCE IS MAINLY DETERMINED BY:

A Our products/services and their quality
B Our internal organization and how we work and provide service
C Our brand and how we are perceived in the markets
D All three of the above

17

ANSWER 1   ANSWER 2

WHICH FIELD IS INDISPENSABLE FOR THE FUTURE OF ORGANIZATIONS TODAY?

A Econometrics
B Psychology
C Philosophy
D Sociology

18

ANSWER 1   ANSWER 2

WHICH OF THE FOLLOWING STATEMENTS BEST FITS US:

A Everyone is aware of their tasks and KPIs
B We make forecasts and adjust along the way
C We can predict the results of our activities in advance
D We have measurement and reporting systems, and we monitor in real-time

19

ANSWER 1   ANSWER 2

WHAT ENSURES YOUR BUSINESS CONTINUITY?

A Data from the recent past
B Current results (the present)
C Looking ahead to the future
D It's difficult or impossible to say

20

ANSWER 1   ANSWER 2

THE SUCCESS OF AN ACTIVITY IS RELATED TO THE FOLLOWING FACTOR:

A Trying to reach as many people as possible in our markets and target groups
B Results measurement
C Predicting prospect conversion and results
D Decisiveness, discipline and perseverance

21

ANSWER 1 ANSWER 2

BUDGETING AND INVESTMENT: HOW DOES OUR ORGANIZATION SPEND ITS MONEY?

A We imitate what the competition does
B We budget a percentage of revenue/profit
C Task-based; we spend what is necessary
D We spend less than what the activity or investment will yield

22

ANSWER 1 ANSWER 2

WHICH OF THE FOLLOWING STATEMENTS ENSURES OUR PROFITABILITY?

A Profit is more important than revenue
B The necessity of ROI (Return On Investment)
C The necessity of Remainder Of Spend
D You have to spend money to make money

23

ANSWER 1 ANSWER 2

WHEN WE DECIDE TO INCUR COSTS:

A We know for sure this will generate more money than the cost
B It's difficult to estimate the return in advance
C We rely on historical experience figures
D It's based on a detailed business case

Your score!

Give 5 points for each correct answer. Your total score reflects the way you currently ensure the continuity and growth of your organization:

1 = C	6 = B	11 = C	16 = D	21 = D
2 = B	7 = C	12 = C	17 = A	22 = C
3 = D	8 = A	13 = A	18 = C	23 = A
4 = B	9 = A	14 = B	19 = B	
5 = C	10 = D	15 = C	20 = C	

115 points	Very good
85 - 115 points	Good
55 - 85 points	Average
30 - 55 points	Poor
< 30 points	Little to no chance of success

ALWAYS SET A CONTINUITY GOAL

AS YOUR STARTING POINT

WITHOUT A GOAL, YOU ACHIEVE NOTHING

Imagine we're meeting for the first time, and we decide to take a walk together. We'd have plenty to discuss, but after a while, you might wonder where we're going. If I responded, 'No idea, I don't have a goal', we could walk for hours, but you'd probably find the walk increasingly less enjoyable. Why? Because we'd never arrive anywhere. We have no goal. Without a goal, you can end up anywhere. With a goal, you arrive at a specific place.

It's essential for everyone and every organization to have a goal, a target. This prevents aimless activity that leads nowhere or, worse, to an undesired destination. Having no goal might seem fine for a while, but it never ends well.

Only 18%

According to research, only 18% of organizations worldwide have set clear goals for themselves. This means a staggering 82% of organizations lack a defined objective. How will they fare in the long run? Remember, if you start the day without an aim, you'll achieve nothing that day.

The Crucial Question

Now, let me ask you a crucial question: What is the objective of your organization? Has it been explicitly outlined? Write it down here:

The goal of my organization is: _____

Now, classify your goal. What category does it fall under? Choose one from the list below. These are the categories into which the objectives typically set by organizations worldwide mostly fall. We'll revisit your selection at the end of this chapter.

Financial   Product development   Sustainability

Marketing   Customer loyalty   New customers

Brand awareness and Reputation   Employee satisfaction

Customer satisfaction   Efficiency   Innovation   Sales

Digital transformation and Technology   Market share

Compliance   Corporate Social Responsibility (CSR)

The Magical Power of Objectives

If you don't know your goal, you won't achieve it. For instance, if you didn't know Amsterdam was your destination, how would you get there? If you don't know where you're going, how will you know what to do in order to arrive at the right place?

An organization that hasn't formulated objectives for itself and its employees won't end up where it needs to be. There's a significant chance it will encounter problems. Without a goal, it will end up doing the wrong things. There's something magical about objectives. They enable you to work out what you need to do to achieve them. Nothing can function without an objective. But simply having a goal isn't enough. If you have the wrong goal in mind, you won't achieve what you want or need.

Before we discuss how to set the right kind of objectives, it's important to understand incorrect objectives. Remember, many organizations struggle with strategic planning and formulating clear goals. This chapter will guide you through this crucial process.

Faulty Objectives

An objective paves the way towards doing what's necessary to achieve it. In fact, a goal directs the activities of organizations and their people. It tells them what they must do. If your goal is wrong, the direction of your activities will also be wrong, leading to disappointing results.

Almost every organization is guilty of formulating incorrect objectives. This is unfortunate because bad objectives always lead to disappointment, while a goal should always bring something positive. A goal should be positive and yield positive results. So let's stop formulating incorrect objectives, starting now.

It's beneficial to first examine the essence of a correct goal. When is something deemed positive? When the outcome is positive. And this is no different for a company, an institution, or any other type of organization.

Despite appearing to be strong brands, well-known names like Polaroid, Woolworth's, Eastman Kodak, General Foods, Lehman Brothers, Motorola, Blockbuster, Pan American World Airways (Pan Am) and many others have disappeared. What went wrong? They made the wrong choices, and this was a result of setting the wrong objectives.

Examples of wrong goals:

- Customer loyalty
- Restyling shops
- Cost-cutting
- Innovation
- Building a strong brand
- Acquiring companies
- Communication campaigns
- Sales promotion
- Obtaining sales appointments
- Introducing new products and services
- Sales objectives
- Stimulating store or website visits
- Marketing measures
- New sales channels
- Increased brand awareness
- Additional services
- Entering new markets

We formulate the wrong goals because we don't know what a correct goal is. The good news (and that's what this book is about) is that it's not necessary for any organization to fail to achieve planned growth, experience hard times, have difficulty making a profit, or be unsuccessful. Just follow my advice, and you'll avoid these pitfalls - simply by correctly formulating your goals and then focusing only on these correct goals.

What is a Correct Goal?

The key to correct goal formulation lies in recognising and avoiding an element common to all incorrectly formulated goals: the fact that they do not offer any guarantee that the organization will survive in a *successful form*. So incorrect goals are those related to shrinking, firing people, reducing costs, etc., in order to survive. These, negative measures are desperate survival mechanisms that will interrupt successful operation.

A correctly formulated goal, on the other hand, is a goal that inherently guarantees the continued success of a *healthy* organization - one that continues without having to resort to negative measures. While some organizations tend to set multiple goals—a topic that has been extensively covered in numerous management books—there is only one, single goal that is truly relevant.

That is the goal that ensures the continuity of your organization. Whether it's a multinational organization or a one-man business, every organization must ensure its continuity. I refer to it as the *continuity goal* - the ultimate destination, the place where you aim to arrive. And from which you can continue!

Continuity has everything to do with 'earning money'. Enough money enables continued, normal, healthy functioning. It's the only sensible option.

A CORRECT GOAL IS A GOAL THAT DEMONSTRABLY RESULTS IN EARNING MONEY FOR THE PURPOSE OF THE CONTINUED EXISTENCE OF A HEALTHY ORGANIZATION.

Use this definition to test your formulated goals. If you are restructuring in order to reduce costs, but as a result will earn less, you are involved in the opposite of continuity: termination.

To revisit what we described above as incorrect goals: you may indeed succeed in innovating new products and services, acquiring companies, achieving marketing goals, creating high brand awareness, or meeting sales objectives - but you may earn nothing or too little in the process. Success is hollow if the result of achieving your goals is insufficient earnings.

CONTINUITY IS ABOUT EARNING ENOUGH MONEY TO COVER ALL EXPENSES, AND PREFERABLY GENERATING ADDITIONAL PROFIT FOR A RESERVE - A 'RAINY DAY' FUND FOR THE FUTURE.

Several renowned frameworks assist organizations in goal-setting. You're probably familiar with some of them. They include the Balanced Scorecard (BSC) by Kaplan and Norton, SMART Goals by Doran, the Stakeholder Theory by R. Edward Freeman, OKR (Objectives and Key Results) by Andy Grove and John Doerr, and Theory of Constraints (TOC) by Eliyahu Goldratt. While these frameworks offer valuable insights – you now no longer need them. For every business, institution, and organization, there is only one, single goal: ensuring continuity.

Continuity is an Element of Growth!

A goal that guarantees continuity of your current situation is a financial growth objective: it involves earning more money. If you earn less than the previous year, your situation worsens. Earning more allows you to absorb rising costs and maintain reserves. Organizations seeking continuity need financial growth objectives - from the smallest to the largest, including non-profits, governments, and even countries!

A charitable institution aimed to fight child abuse globally. They initially viewed earning money as taboo. When asked how they fought child abuse in practice, they replied, 'By having projects on every continent'. These projects, of course, required money from donations – measured in millions. I asked, 'What would happen if you didn't receive the necessary funds?'

After a pause, they admitted they would then not be able to run their projects or fight child abuse. I then asked, 'So, what's your real goal?' The answer then became clear: to earn the money necessary to run their projects. They then identified a need for 20% growth, which became their Bitsing goal. They achieved this goal within three months, and doubled their donations within a year - simply by making earning money their goal.

When an organization knows what it must earn, it can plan how to earn it. A financial growth objective is the only correct goal for every organization. Everything you and your organization do should start with determining how much money you need to earn. From now on, I'll refer to this targeted amount as 'turnover' or 'revenue', i.e. the total amount of money received by an organisation, from all sources.

It's About a Specific Amount of Money

Did you formulate a goal at the beginning of this chapter? If so, does it guarantee your organization's continuity? In other words, is it a specific amount of turnover? Yes, the correct category for your goal should be 'financial.'

Ask your colleagues and employees what goal they'd set for your organization. Their answers will probably include everything except continuity-related goals: 'To be the best', 'retain clients', 'become market leader', 'survive', 'grow', 'deliver quality', 'streamline distribution', etc.

Even vague financial terms like 'more turnover', 'profit', and '5% turnover growth' are inadequate. The issue is, how much money is 5%? Make your continuity goal tangible by expressing it as a specific amount of money.

Example — The incorrect objective of a telecom company

A telecom company aimed to acquire 700,000 new subscribers. When they applied Bitsing and formulated a continuity turnover goal, they realized they needed 900,000 new customers to guarantee sustainability. The company wouldn't have survived with its previous, incorrect objective.

Make Revenue not Profit your Goal

Why prioritise revenue over profit as a continuity goal? It's simple. There's no profit without revenue. You need turnover to make a profit - not vice versa. Focus on turnover when setting your goal, not profit. We'll address profit later in this book.

Defining the Continuity Revenue Goal

The first step towards becoming a financially successful organisation is formulating a continuity revenue or turn-over goal. We will define this for your organisation (or business unit, local government or company department).

The turnover goal can be any amount, but the minimum requirement is the amount that guarantees continuity – in the above sense of sustaining your business in a healthy state. I cannot emphasize this enough. A wide variety of turnover goals have been achieved by applying the Bitsing method, ranging from very low for recently started businesses to many billions for multinationals. Even the GNP (gross national product) of a country is turnover and must be earned by its residents.

Start by defining the period in which you need to earn the required turnover. This is preferably, and frequently, the twelve-month period commencing from when you start to apply the Bitsing method. Now formulate the goal you need to achieve to continue operating. Determine three goals:

The real continuity goal

The target revenue needed to cover
all expense, including rising costs.

The ambition goal

A slightly higher amount based on your desired growth,
including a suitable amount to cover profit.

The dream goal

The revenue target that could be achieved
if everything goes perfectly.

Most organisations that implement Bitsing achieve increased revenue that falls between the ambition and dream goals.

ALWAYS DOUBLE-CHECK THE ACCURACY OF YOUR DETERMINED, TARGET AMOUNT.

Example The Bitsing continuity goal of a toy retailer

I once asked a prominent toy retailer about his turnover goal for the upcoming twelve months. He replied, '530 million euros.' When I inquired about his earnings from the comparable, previous twelve-month period, he gave the same answer: '530 million euros.' I challenged him, 'But that's exactly the same amount. Is that correct? Haven't your costs increased? If so, doesn't that mean your turnover goal of 530 million euros would never cover all your costs, potentially forcing you to reduce staff?'

The retailer admitted he was already downsizing and would be content to earn 530 million euros again, given extreme pressures in the market and declining sales. I disagreed. When you apply Bitsing, you set goals that *ensure your organisation's continuity – not its decline*.

I asked the retailer what turnover would be necessary for his business to continue functioning in its current form while also generating a healthy profit. He answered, 'It should be 600 million euros.' This became his Bitsing continuity goal.

The result? The toy retailer actually achieved growth exceeding 30% (from 530 to 690.7 million euros), while his two direct competitors suffered declines of about 8% in turnover. He outperformed them by at least 39%.

This example illustrates the power of setting the right continuity goal and refusing to be limited by perceived market constraints. It demonstrates how the Bitsing method can drive significant growth, even in challenging market conditions.

> Surprise yourself! Before you start with the next chapter, I would like you to answer a question. You'll find it at www.bitsing.com/growth. It will take you a few seconds to answer this question. Do it before you continue with chapter 2.
> At the end of this book, you'll make use of this answer – and you'll be surprised at what this reveals about happened to you as a result of the Bitsing method. This result will motivate you for the rest of your life.

Many organisations, particularly start-ups or smaller businesses, struggle with strategic planning and formulating clear goals. This chapter aims to guide you through this crucial process and set you on the path to achieving your continuity goals through the Bitsing method.

Be Inspired

Here are the key practical examples from chapter 1, briefly summarized:

The aimless walk: this chapter opens with a hypothetical scenario of a walk without a destination, illustrating the futility of action without a clear goal.

The charitable institution: a charity fighting child abuse initially resisted the idea of a financial goal. After adopting a revenue target (20% growth), they doubled their donations within a year, enabling more effective pursuit of their mission.

The telecom company: a telecom company had set a goal of acquiring 700,000 new subscribers. After applying Bitsing and formulating a continuity turnover goal, they realized they actually needed 900,000 new customers to ensure survival.

The toy retailer: A famous toy retailer aimed to maintain the previous year's turnover of €530 million, despite rising costs. After applying Bitsing principles and setting a continuity goal of €600 million, they achieved over 30% growth (€690.7 million), outperforming competitors with sales that declined by 8%.

These examples demonstrate:

1	The importance of having a clear, financial goal
2	How setting the right goal can dramatically improve performance
3	The potential for growth even in challenging market conditions
4	The value of focusing on revenue to ensure continuity
5	How the Bitsing method can help you exceed your initial expectations

These real-world cases serve as powerful motivators, showing that with the right approach to goal-setting, organisations can achieve significant growth and ensure their continuity.

PITFALLS THREATENING THE CONTINUITY OF ORGANISATIONS

These pitfalls underscore the importance of setting clear, measurable, financial continuity goals as the foundation for an organisation's success and sustainability. By avoiding these common traps, organisations can better ensure their long-term viability and growth.

1 **Lack of a clear goal:** organisations without a defined objective risk operating aimlessly and never reaching any destination.

2 **Setting incorrect goals:** focusing on goals that don't directly contribute to the organisation's continuity, such as cost-cutting or innovation without financial context.

3 **Pursuing multiple, unrelated goals:** this can lead to fragmentation of resources and attention.

4 **Setting non-financial goals as primary objectives:** for example, focusing solely on customer satisfaction or market share without linking these to financial outcomes.

5 **Accepting stagnation:** being content with the same revenue level as previous years, without accounting for rising costs.

6 **Short-term thinking:** focusing on survival rather than continuity and growth.

7 **Using market conditions as an excuse:** blaming the market for poor performance instead of taking proactive action.

8 **Prioritising profitability over revenue:** forgetting that sufficient revenue is necessary before profit can be made.

9 **Setting vague or unmeasurable goals:** such as 'wanting to be the best' without quantifying this ambition.

10 **Failing to distinguish between continuity, ambition, and dream goals:** this causes you to miss the opportunity to be both realistic and ambitious.

11 **Not communicating goals:** if employees don't know or understand the goals, they can't effectively contribute to them.

12 **Neglecting financial growth:** forgetting that growth is necessary to absorb rising costs and build reserves.

THE LEARNINGS FROM THIS CHAPTER

The Do's

1 Set a clear, specific continuity goal for your organisation. **2** Express your continuity goal as a concrete amount of money (revenue). **3** Define your goal for a specific period, preferably 12 months. **4** Formulate three levels of goals: Continuity, Ambition, and Dream. **5** Ensure your continuity goal covers all expenses, including rising costs. **6** Focus on revenue first, then profit. **7** Regularly review and adjust your goals to ensure they still guarantee continuity. **8** Communicate your continuity goal clearly to all employees. **9** Use your continuity goal to guide all organisational activities and decisions. **10** Aim for financial growth to absorb rising costs and build reserves.

THE LEARNINGS FROM THIS CHAPTER

The Don'ts

1 Don't operate without a clearly defined goal. **2** Avoid setting non-financial objectives as your primary goals (e.g., market share, customer satisfaction). **3** Don't confuse tasks or activities (like marketing or innovation) with actual goals. **4** Avoid setting multiple, unrelated goals that may fragment your focus. **5** Don't accept stagnation or decline as inevitable due to market conditions. **6** Avoid setting vague or unmeasurable goals like 'being the best'. **7** Don't prioritise cost-cutting over revenue growth as a primary strategy. **8** Avoid focusing solely on short-term survival at the expense of long-term continuity. **9** Don't set a goal that's the same as last year's revenue without accounting for increased costs. **10** Avoid setting profit as your primary goal before ensuring sufficient revenue.

Remember: a correct goal is one that demonstrably results in earning money for the purpose of the continued existence of a healthy organisation. Always check if your goal guarantees the continuity of your organisation in its current form.

YOU WILL REACH YOUR GOAL

IF YOU MOVE IN THE RIGHT DIRECTION

GUARANTEE YOUR SUCCESS BY FOCUSSING ON HARD FINANCIAL FACTS

Now that you've identified your goal, I'll show you why you can be 100% certain of achieving it, overcoming any obstacles along the way. In this inspiring chapter, I'll demonstrate that reaching goals easily is a matter of making the right choices. I'll share how nothing can fail anymore, and how success is guaranteed.

The models presented here will show how you can achieve even the most ambitious growth objectives while expending less effort and money. Do you want to benefit yourself and those around you with a 25% saving in time and money while reaching ambitious revenue growth goals? With Bitsing this is the rule, not the exception.

In chapter 1, we established that everything revolves around achieving the turnover goal that secures your organisation's ongoing, healthy existence: the continuity turnover goal. Ideally, you'll reach the Ambition turnover goal and strive for the dream turnover goal.

Research Insights:

According to Harvard Business Review, approximately 95% of employees lack a complete understanding of their organisation's strategy.

Forbes indicates that 84% of organisations do not effectively utilise data to measure and enhance their performance.

A Gallup report shows only 41% of employees feel connected to their organisation's mission or purpose.

These statistics highlight the need for clear goal-setting and effective communication within organisations.

Still not sure about how to 'mine' data, apply the results - or even whether it's worth the effort? Learn how to simply transcend the whole issue - with Bitsing.

The value of a goal lies in successfully achieving it. So, we want certainty that we'll meet our continuity goal, and even our ambition and dream goals!

NEVER DO WHAT YOU THINK YOU SHOULD DO, BECAUSE A THOUGHT IS JUST AN ASSUMPTION.

To illustrate this point, gather a small group of friends or colleagues. Tell them you want to travel to Amsterdam and ask for their advice on which direction to go. Each is likely to point in a different direction, demonstrating the unreliability of assumptions when the goal isn't visible.

The Truth is in the Facts

You've undoubtedly heard the saying, 'facts don't lie'. Facts are demonstrably correct. Assumptions are not. The truth is thus based on fact. So why base your choices and decisions on assumptions? The chances of achieving your goal are much greater if you base your decisions on facts.

What makes the Bitsing method special is that you'll no longer base your decisions on assumptions, but purely on facts. Feeding the methods and models of Bitsing with factual information means that factual answers and solutions will emerge. These, if acted upon, will lead to factual, and thus guaranteed, results!

FEEDING THE METHODS
AND MODELS OF BITSING
WITH FACTUAL INFORMATION
MEANS THAT FACTUAL
ANSWERS AND SOLUTIONS
WILL EMERGE. AND THUS,
GUARANTEED RESULTS!

The Pitfall

Imagine we're in a casino, at the roulette table. We start by putting a chip on black or red. I think we should bet on red. However, if you know in advance that the roulette ball will land on black, would you place your chip on red?

Bitsing offers inspiring solutions, but it can sometimes ask you to act counter-intuitively. What you have to do is not always what you want to do or what you're used to doing. Regardless of how factually correct an outcome may be, it doesn't always feel comfortable. Opinions based on facts may well be at odds with what one is used to.

What is Factual Information?

This is primarily information based on demonstrable truths, not visions, thoughts, or wishes. It's simply information as it is, not as it seems. The ideal information for application in the Bitsing method is current information. Today's information. Not yesterday's (that's over, gone), and not tomorrow's (which is an expectation, an assumption).

Focus, Focus, Focus

The information in the upcoming pages lays the groundwork for problem-free achievement of your turnover goals. This starts with understanding what you should focus on and where to direct your efforts. I'm going to start by forcing you to make choices. You can't do everything, let alone focus your attention, money, and time on everything. So let's focus on what's critical for achieving success.

The Criteria for Correct Choices

Choices cannot be based on mere feeling. If you navigate a boat across the ocean purely on feeling, reaching your destination will be a matter of chance.

Choices (and focus) are about maximising chances. Why waste precious time, human resources, and money on something if you're not sure it will bring you closer to your goal? The right choices are those that you're (demonstrably) sure will enable you to achieve your turnover goal.

To make the right choices, look at your *type* of goal. The right choices for achieving a revenue goal will always have a *financial* aspect. After all, a financial goal is what you're aiming to achieve.

The Pencils Philosophy

This is a significant section. It covers a tool I invented that has both helped many organisations succeed and prevented major financial debacles: the Pencils Philosophy.

The Pencils Philosophy focuses you and your choices on the things that make the achievement of your goal certain. It very simply and clearly identifies your priorities and the amount of attention you must pay to each of them. It indicates how you must allocate your time and guides your financial investment. It even makes the correct set-up of your internal organisation a piece of cake. In fact, the Pencils Philosophy will interrogate the strategy of your entire organisation.

Take six pencils. Three are more blunt and three are sharper, all to varying degrees. Line them up, with the bluntest on the extreme left and the sharpest on the extreme right. If you had to write down your turnover goal (see chapter 1), which pencil would you choose? You'd avoid the blunt ones, right?

This reveals something significant: the choice isn't about the pencil, but whether it has a point or not.

SUCCESS IS ABOUT THE POINT, NOT THE PENCIL.

The sharper the pencil, the more you can write with it. The blunt pencils will always disappoint. Of course you could sharpen one of the blunter pencils. But that will take time – before you can write successfully and continuously with it, as with the sharper pencils on the right side. The pencils symbolise the choices you make to achieve your turnover goal. One option will bring you closer to achieving your target than another.

The Money Sources

Your first step is to look at the factors that *directly* influence achievement of your turnover goal: the turnover determinants. Or as I call them the *money sources*. The money sources are the sources that are demonstrably sure to generate revenue. These are the sources from which revenue undeniably originates. Not the means through which or with which your revenue is generated, but the sources in which your money is generated.

Which of the following are your actual 'money sources'? Where are you currently generating your money? From:

Continents?

Countries?

Regions?

Markets (i.e., consumers, governments, etc.)?

Industries (i.e., financial, automotive, corporates, etc.)?

Target groups (i.e., 60-plus, Generation Z, CEOs, etc.)?

Decision-makers (by job function)?

Brands?

Product categories?

Products/services?

Sales channels?

Particular seasons?

Or periods (months, weeks, etc.)?

Other money sources?

Don't forget to add your own success-defining money sources.

Making the Right Choices Based on the Pencils Philosophy

Consider all your listed turnover determinants, your money sources, and the obstacles to achieving turnover, one by one. Each offers you the opportunity to make choices on which to focus – from 'sharp pencil' choices to the bluntest pencil. The choice of, and thus the focus on, sharp pencils will immediately lead to positive results. Revenue! These choices will help you achieve your turnover target. While selecting blunt pencils will minimise your chances of success.

What defines a 'sharp pencil' choice, and what doesn't?

Example · A supermarket's product strategy

A supermarket has six products on the shelf, each achieving a certain turnover:

Product	Turnover
A	€10,000
B	€5,000
C	€330,000
D	€100,000
E	€120,000
F	€94,000

Arrange these products in order of priority, based on their share of turnover:

	Product	Turnover	Share
1	C	€330,000	50%
2	E	€120,000	18%
3	D	€100,000	15%
4	F	€94,000	14%
5	A	€10,000	2%
6	B	€5,000	1%

How should the supermarket match its products to the pencils? The products represented by sharp pencils (C, E, and D) make up more than 60% of the turnover. The last three products are blunt pencils, representing a minor part of the turnover. The product that has achieved the most turnover – Product C – is given highest priority. The product with the lowest turnover – product B – gets the lowest priority.

Try This Exercise for Yourself

How are your products and services distributed in terms of revenue? What's their priority and current share of revenue? If you have more than six products, categorise them into overarching categories.

Focus on Hard Financial Facts and Don't Deviate from Them

The choices you make must serve to maximize turnover opportunities. Turnover is a financial measure. If you want to maximise your chances of higher turnover, test your choices against the turnover achieved in an earlier period. This is the hardest financial fact in your possession.

Start-ups need to get information about the market, similar organisations, and from competitors, using internet and AI tools. Over time, you'll acquire more data about your own situation, which will drive your progress.

Example A car dealer's sharp pencil

A car dealer turning over €330 million faces a declining market. He considers selling electric bikes. The product is new to him and he plans to focus all his attention on electric bikes sales. What are his chances of maintaining his turnover? Not high. Car sales are his sharp pencil. The advice: focus mainly on car sales, gradually increasing attention to electric bikes as their turnover grows.

FACTS DON'T LIE, BASE YOUR CHOICES ON FACTS AND YOUR GOALS WILL BE WITHIN REACH

Developing a Turnover Growth Strategy

The Pencils Philosophy not only prioritises your options but also indicates how much attention each choice needs. Have a look at the supermarket example on the previous page again. The percentages at the right indicate the attention required per product. For instance, about 50% of the supermarket's focus should be on Product C. And so on. This simplifies the business of focusing your attention (and that of all others in your organisation) enormously.

How do you apply a 50% focus to a €100,000 investment, a 40-hour work week, and a team of 10 employees? Simple: allocate €50,000, 20 hours, and 5 employees to Product C.

Refining Your Growth Strategy

The degree of attention doesn't have to match the turnover share exactly. If there's a downward trend in the demand for products like C and F because they are unprofitable and/or ageing you might give them slightly less attention. Conversely, products with growth and profit potential (A and B) could receive more attention. This is called 'sharpening the pencils'.

The 5% rule

Scientific studies on the Bitsing method revealed a valuable guideline for adjusting the allocation of attention:

> Increase focus by 5% for 'pencils' representing potential growth areas and profit generators.

> Decrease focus by 5% for 'pencils' that are declining or unprofitable.

> Maintain the current focus percentage for other 'pencils', in line with their share of turnover.

This 5% rule provides a balanced approach to resource allocation, allowing you to nurture growth opportunities while gradually reducing investment in underperforming areas. It ensures that you're continuously optimising your focus, without making drastic changes that could destabilise your business.

By implementing this strategy over a short period (e.g. three to six months) and then reassessing, you can fine-tune your approach based on real-world results.

This approach of incremental adjustment aligns perfectly with the Bitsing philosophy of making decisions based on hard financial facts, ensuring that your strategy evolves in tandem with your business performance.

The growth strategy of the supermarket:

	Product	Turnover	Share	Growth Strategy	New Focus
B	C	€330,000	50%	-/- 5%	45%
I	E	€120,000	18%	Neutral	18%
T	D	€100,000	15%	Neutral	15%
S	F	€94,000	14%	-/- 5%	9%
E	A	€10,000	2%	+ 5%	7%
R	B	€5,000	1%	+ 5%	6%

Don't overdo it. Ensure the attention given remains close to each product's actual turnover share. This allows you to grow new 'blunt' products without risk, while safely reducing focus on declining products.

The Role of Blunt Pencil Choices

While sharp pencil choices lead to immediate achievement of turnover goals, blunt pencils ensure future continuity. They often represent new products, services, markets, or channels. Don't make the mistake of only focusing on blunt pencils, but don't neglect them either.

Applying the Pencil Philosophy

Use the achieved turnover as your factual touchstone. This is the cornerstone of the Bitsing method's fact-based approach. This is the turnover earned in the comparable period preceding your goal period, such as:

> The previous calendar year

> The last twelve months (rolling annual turnover)

> The same quarter or month from the previous year, if your business is highly seasonal

For a business, it's the total of all invoices; for a government, total tax revenue; for a charity, donations. This achieved turnover provides a solid, factual basis for your decision-making. It's not a projection or an aspiration. It's a specific reflection of your business's actual performance. By using this as your reference point, you ground all your strategic decisions in reality, rather than assumptions.

Remember, the goal is to work with the most current data possible. While the previous year's total can be useful for annual planning, using the most recent twelve months' data (updated monthly) can provide an even more current picture of your business trends, especially in rapidly changing markets. This approach ensures that your 'pencils' are always selected and, where applicable sharpened based on the most relevant financial facts available, allowing you to adapt your strategy in real-time to changing business conditions.

Applying the Pencils Philosophy to the Other Money Sources

Let's apply the Pencils Philosophy to turnover using, as an example, turnover per continent:

1	List the continents
2	Write down the achieved turnover per continent
3	Calculate each continent's percentage share of turnover
4	Rank the continents in order of share of turnover
5	Analyse the continent growth strategy
6	Round off percentages and allocate focus accordingly

	Turnover	Share	Growth Strategy	New Focus	Rounded
1	€53,500,000	34%	-/- 5%	29%	30%
2	€47,000,000	30%	+ 5%	35%	35%
3	€31,000,000	20%	Neutral	20%	20%
4	€16,000,000	10%	- 5%	5%	5%
5	€8,000,000	5%	+ 5%	10%	10%
6	€1,500,000	1%	Neutral	1%	0%

1	Europe	**4**	South America
2	North America	**5**	Africa
3	Asia	**6**	Australia

Europe, North America and Asia currently account for 84% share of turnover. These are the sharp pencils. Apply this process to other money sources to gain fact-based insights into which areas should dominate your focus.

Determining the Revenue Target for Each Money Source

To set precise revenue targets for your money sources, follow these steps:

1   Refer to your overall revenue goal from chapter 1, your turnover goal.

2   Review the new focus percentages you've assigned to each money source based on the Pencils Philosophy.

3   Calculate the revenue target for each money source by applying its focus percentage to your overall revenue goal.

For example:

Overall revenue goal: €1,000,000

Money source A focus: 50%

Money source A revenue target:
50% of €1,000,000 = €500,000

This method ensures that your revenue targets for individual money sources align with your overall goal and reflect the strategic focus you've determined. It provides clear, quantifiable objectives for each area of your business, allowing for more precise planning and performance measurement.

By setting specific targets for each money source, you create a roadmap for achieving your overall revenue goal, with each component playing its designated role in your business's success.

The Nursery

The leftmost blunt pencil is the 'nursery'. Here, you place all money sources currently generating less than 5% of your turnover or no turnover at all. From this nursery, select one money source to develop. Give it 5% of your attention (no more) and monitor its growth. This nursery concept balances current performance with future potential. It allows you to nurture new revenue streams without neglecting your top performers.

By limiting focus to 5%, you invest in the future responsibly. Remember, today's nursery item could become tomorrow's sharp pencil. This systematic approach increases your chances of identifying and developing new successful revenue streams while maintaining focus on current drivers.

Inspiration from Real-World Applications

An international airport: a simple switch in target group and product focus achieved record turnover for shops in a top-ten international airport.

An American toy store: by identifying fathers as the primary paying customers (the 'money target group') and adjusting marketing accordingly, a toy chain reversed declining sales to achieve 30% growth while competitors declined by 18%.

A mobile telephony leader: removing their most popular subscription plan (200 minutes) in hopes of upselling customers backfired, resulting in customers downgrading to the smallest plan. The Pencils Philosophy could have predicted this outcome.

Your Organisation's Efficiency

The Pencils Philosophy can reveal inefficiencies in your organisation. For example, if 80% of your turnover comes from the consumer market, but only 20% of your staff works in that department, you may need to reallocate resources.

A financial institution found that 4% of its turnover came from 43% of its customers, yet half the employees worked on these 'blunt pencil' customers. A simple reorganisation reduced workload pressure and grew turnover by 25%.

Finally

If your choices deliver disappointing results, you're likely to be putting too much focus on 'blunt pencil' options. For success, a 'sharp pencil' choice is indicated. Always ask, 'Am I using a sharp pencil or a blunt one?'

The Best Decision-Making Tool

Imagine three gifts made of paper: toilet paper, printer paper and a roll of money. Which would you choose? Most people choose the money, demonstrating that adding the word 'money' to a decision makes the choice clearer! Apply this to your business decisions. Is it 'social media' or 'money social media'? An 'online shop' or a 'money online shop'? Similar comparisons can be made across various aspects of your business:

A region vs. a money region

A target group vs. a money target group

A decision-maker vs. a money decision-maker

Products vs. money products

A department vs. a money department

A competitor vs. a money competitor

This simple tool can streamline your decision-making process, ensuring you focus on what truly contributes to your financial goals. Remember: In the world of business, clarity is power. And nothing provides more clarity than decisions based on cold, hard facts. To ensure that you focus on facts when making decisions, frequently ask yourself the question: 'Do I think this is true, or do I know this is true?'

Key Learnings: The Power of Fact-Based Decision Making

By internalising and applying these key learnings, you're not just aiming for success - you're guaranteeing it. The Bitsing method, with its focus on hard financial facts and strategic allocation of resources, provides a clear, actionable path to achieving your most ambitious business goals.

1

Facts over assumptions:
The cornerstone of success is basing decisions on hard financial facts rather than assumptions or gut feelings. This approach dramatically increases your chances of achieving your goals.

2

The Pencils Philosophy:
Visualise your choices as pencils. Sharp pencils represent high-performing areas that deserve more focus, while blunt ones may need less attention or development over time.

3

Turnover is king:
Focus on turnover as your primary financial metric. It's the clearest indicator of your business's health and potential for growth.

4

Prioritise your focus:
Allocate your attention, resources, and efforts according to the 'sharpness' of each business area. Typically, 60-80% of your focus should be on your top-performing segments.

5

Adapt dynamically:
Regularly reassess your 'pencils' and adjust your focus. What's sharp now may become blunt over time, and vice versa.

6

The money perspective:
Frame your decisions by adding the word 'money' to your options. This simple trick can clarify which choices truly contribute to your financial goals.

7

Organisational efficiency:
Use the Pencils Philosophy to optimise your organisational structure, ensuring resources are allocated where they can make the most impact.

8

Start-up strategy:
For new businesses, use market data and competitor information to inform your decisions, while you build your own, historical data.

9

Balanced growth:
While focusing on your 'sharp pencils', don't neglect your 'blunt' ones entirely. They often represent future growth opportunities.

10

Continuous measurement:
Regularly measure your performance against these principles to ensure you're on track to meet and exceed your goals.

PITFALLS THREATENING ORGANISATIONAL CONTINUITY AND GROWTH

By being aware of the pitfalls and actively working to avoid them, you can maintain continuity and foster sustainable growth of your business. Remember, the key to success lies in making decisions based on hard financial facts and continuously aligning your focus with your proven revenue generators.

1 **Assumption-based decision making:** relying on gut feel or assumptions rather than hard financial facts can lead to misguided strategies and wasted resources.

2 **Neglecting top performers:** taking your most successful products, services or markets (your 'sharp pencils') for granted can result in declining performance in your core business areas.

3 **Over-investing in underperformers:** allocating disproportionate resources to struggling segments ('blunt pencils') at the expense of high-performing areas can drain your organisation's potential for growth.

4 **Resistance to change:** clinging to outdated strategies or business models, even when financial data suggests they're no longer effective, can hinder adaptation to market changes.

5 **Misalignment of organisational structure:** failing to align your organisational structure with your revenue-generating activities can lead to inefficiencies and missed opportunities.

6 **Chasing trends without financial justification:** pursuing new initiatives or technologies without clear evidence of their potential return on investment can divert resources from proven revenue streams.

7 **Ignoring market saturation:** failing to recognize when a product or market is reaching its growth limit can result in diminishing returns and missed opportunities for diversification.

8 **Misinterpreting financial data:** drawing incorrect conclusions from financial facts due to lack of context or misunderstanding can lead to poor strategic decisions.

9 **Short-term focus:** prioritising short-term gains at the expense of long-term sustainability and growth can jeopardize the organisation's future.

10 **Overlooking competitive threats:** failing to monitor and respond to competitive pressures can result in loss of market share and declining revenues.

11 **Inconsistent performance measurement:** not regularly assessing the performance of different aspects of business can allow inefficiencies to persist and opportunities to be missed.

12 **Ignoring customer payment behaviour:** focusing marketing efforts on product users rather than actual paying customers (as in the toy store example) can result in misdirected resources and missed sales opportunities.

13 **Drastic strategy shifts:** making sudden, large-scale changes to your business strategy without thorough analysis of potential impacts on turnover can disrupt successful operations and customer relationships.

14 **Overcomplicating decision-making:** using overly complex models or considering too many variables when making business decisions can lead to 'analysis paralysis' and missed opportunities.

15 **Neglecting future growth opportunities:** while focusing on your current, top performers is crucial, completely ignoring potential future revenue sources ('blunt pencils') can leave your organisation vulnerable to market shifts and new competitors.

THE LEARNINGS FROM THIS CHAPTER

The Do's

1 Base decisions on hard financial facts, not assumptions. **2** Apply the Pencils Philosophy to prioritise and allocate attention. **3** Focus primarily on turnover as the key financial indicator. **4** Dedicate 60-80% of your attention to your best-performing segments ('sharp pencils'). **5** Regularly re-evaluate your 'pencils' and adjust your focus accordingly. **6** Use the 'money' perspective when making choices (e.g., 'money social media' vs. 'money online shop'). **7** Optimize your organisational structure based on the Pencils Philosophy. **8** For start-ups: use market data and competitor information until you have your own historical data. **9** Pay some attention to 'blunt pencils' as future growth opportunities. **10** Continuously measure your performance against these principles.

THE LEARNINGS FROM THIS CHAPTER

The Don'ts

1 Don't rely on intuition or gut feelings when making important decisions. **2** Don't ignore hard financial facts, even if they don't align with your expectations. **3** Don't give equal attention to all aspects of your business; prioritise based on turnover contribution. **4** Don't completely neglect your underperforming segments ('blunt pencils'). **5** Don't cling to strategies that no longer work, even if they were successful in the past. **6** Don't get distracted by non-financial metrics when making financial decisions. **7** Don't overestimate the importance of new, unproven initiatives at the expense of existing successful activities. **8** Don't make drastic decisions without first analysing the impact on your turnover. **9** Don't ignore signs that a 'sharp pencil' is becoming blunt. **10** Don't forget to regularly recalibrate your strategy based on current financial data.

These do's and don'ts summarize the core principles of the Bitsing method as presented in this chapter. They offer you a practical checklist to improve their decision-making and strategies.

EVERYTHING THAT'S COPYABLE

IS LESS
APPEALING

YOU ARE UNBEATABLE

How do you beat your competitors? Can you remove all obstacles to achieving your turnover target? These questions seem unanswerable, but there are answers, and you'll soon have them. Winning market share starts with defeating everything that obstructs you. The key is 'being unbeatable'. Only when you're unbeatable can you be sure you'll always emerge victorious, overcoming every obstacle.

With this third law of the Bitsing method, I'll take you on an amazing journey in which you'll discover how your organisation can become unbeatable. This will take you less than two hours, without requiring that you change anything. Because you're already unbeatable; you just don't know why yet.

Organisations often spend fortunes on consultants to identify their unique selling points and develop complex strategies. These processes can take months and often yield little value. We'll take a different approach, revealing the foundation of 'unbeatability' and translating it into appropriate organisational and marketing strategies - all in a matter of hours.

The Eight Learnings of Unbeatability

Decades of research and practical applications across thousands of projects have shown that unbeatability rests on eight learnings:

1	Overcome barriers, not problems
2	Always focus on three barriers
3	Formulate the right barrier focus strategy
4	Develop three forms of policy
5	Focus on a different competitor
6	Use the right content for the right policy
7	Create the correct market proposition
8	Be uncopyable

Let's examine each pillar in detail.

1

Overcome barriers, not problems

Unbeatability begins with overcoming barriers, not solving internal problems. The only real barriers to achieving your turn-over goal reside in your target group. If these barriers didn't exist, everyone would be your customer and you'd have long since achieved your continuity turnover target.

Yet many organisations prioritise their own problems above market barriers. Most marketing campaigns communicate the organisation's problems instead of addressing customer obstacles. For example:

> **'Big discounts'** - We have a sales problem.

> **'Tell others how good we are'** - We lack word-of-mouth advertising.

> **'We are honest'** - We've been involved in a scandal.

> **'Take a test drive'** - We have too few showroom visits.

> **'The best service'** - Keep hoping for it.

Almost all marketing campaigns expose the advertiser's problem. But who wants to hear about someone else's problems? Instead, focus on removing barriers for your customers.

2

Always focus on three barriers

In every market and target group, you encounter three barriers:

1 **The preference barrier:**
Those who 'don't want' your product or service.

2 **The buying behaviour barrier:**
Those who want but 'don't buy'.

3 **The loyalty barrier:**
Those who have bought but 'don't stay'.

The Preference Barrier
Someone must first want your brand before they can consider purchase. If you're not on their preference list, they'll never buy you. Preference doesn't guarantee purchase, but it's the foundation for it.

The Buying Behaviour Barrier
Even among those who prefer your brand, buying behaviour doesn't follow automatically. You must stimulate purchases among those who want your product but haven't bought yet.

The Loyalty Barrier
There's always a group of people who've made a one-time purchase but don't continue buying. They become one-time buyers and may eventually become someone else's customers. This barrier applies to existing customers who lack the loyalty to maintain the relationship.

The Best Strategy: Focus on All Three Barriers

Your organisation should pursue three strategies simultaneously:

1	A strategy focused on preference
2	A strategy focused on buying behaviour
3	A strategy focused on customer loyalty

Most organisations primarily focus on stimulating buying behaviour and neglect preference and loyalty. This approach misses significant opportunities.

For example, imagine that, out of 100 people:

10 are already customers

30 prefer your brand but haven't bought yet

60 don't prefer your brand

If you focus only on buying behaviour, you're targeting just 30 people and missing 70 (your 10 existing customers plus the 60 who don't prefer you). Products and services encourage buying behaviour; brands stimulate preference. If your organisation primarily communicates about its products or services, it's missing the chance to build brand preference.

3

Formulate the right barrier focus strategy

The extent to which each barrier plays a role in your markets and target groups will determine your focus strategy. This will be discussed in chapter 4, with the BITSER steps.

4

Develop three forms of policy

To achieve preference, buying behaviour and loyalty in your markets and target groups, focus your organisation according to the emphases prescribed by the barrier focus strategy in chapter 4:

1 **Preference policy:** focuses on your brand

2 **Buying behaviour policy:** focuses on your product/service

3 **Loyalty policy:** focuses on your internal organisation

How Preference Works

To do business with someone, they must first want you - have a preference for you. If you're not on their list of preferred brands, you'll never be bought. It's that simple.

Think about your own behaviour. When choosing a car, fashion label, perfume or supplier, how many brands make it onto your preference list? Not all of them, right? People often have multiple preferences, shopping around and considering alternatives.

Preference doesn't guarantee a purchase, but without it, a purchase is virtually impossible. It's like politics - you need to want a certain party before you'll vote for them. Preference is the foundation for any transaction. In this book, when we talk about getting someone to 'buy' or 'purchase', we're really talking about getting them to do what you want them to do. And it all starts with preference.

How Purchasing Behavior Works

Now, let's be clear: someone without a preference for you won't buy from you. Period. But here's the thing - even among those who prefer you, automatic purchases are rare. Buying behaviour doesn't just happen; you need to make it happen.

For those who don't prefer you yet, your first job is to develop that preference. But what about those who do prefer you, but aren't buying? You need to stimulate buying behaviour. This is where you start recruiting new customers. Preference is just the first step. Turning that preference into action is where the real work begins.

How Loyalty Works

Here's a hard truth: there's always a group of people who've bought from you once, but don't come back. They're one-time buyers who drift away, often becoming someone else's loyal customers. This is the loyalty barrier, and it applies to your existing customers. They've bought from you, sure, but they lack the loyalty to maintain the relationship and keep doing what you ask of them. Loyalty isn't a given. It's something you need to cultivate continuously, even after the sale. Because in business, as in life, it's not just about winning people over - it's about keeping the relationship going.

5

Focus on the *real* competitor

Your competitor isn't who you think it is. The key to invincibility lies in redefining your competitive landscape. Here's why:

A customer's money can only be spent once. But who are you really competing with for that spend? Let's challenge your assumptions with a real-world example.

An animal park saw other parks and zoos as competitors. They invested heavily in analysing these 'rivals'. But their analysis missed the mark entirely. I asked them two simple questions:

1   **'Out of 100 potential customers, how many buy tickets to your park?'** Answer: one.

2   **'How many buy tickets to other parks or zoos?'** Answer: four.

This left 95 (100 -/- 1 -/- 4) people spending their money elsewhere. The park's real competition wasn't other animal attractions - it was whatever these 95 people were choosing to spend their money on instead.

Further investigation revealed the unexpected answer: toys. People were spending their entertainment budget on toys rather than park visits. This revelation transformed the park's strategy. They started competing with toy companies, offering free toys with ticket purchases and making themselves the unbeatable alternative to toys.

The result? By recognizing this, the park doubled their revenue, capturing two customers out of every hundred instead of just one. The park's real competitor wasn't other animal parks, but toys – the alternative on which most people were spending their money. The lesson? Don't fixate on obvious competitors. Your real competition is often the alternative way people could spend their money - what we call the 'money competitor'. By understanding and addressing this, you can tap into massive growth potential you never knew existed.

6

Use the right content for the right policy

Your policy content is derived from two aspects:

1	What your brand, product, and organisation mean to your target group(s)
2	What you have to offer them - your proposition

Brand Meaning
Your brand's meaning relates to its purpose in society. Don't mention the product when communicating your brand's purpose. A brand's purpose is the subject matter for its preference policy.

Product/Service Meaning
Products and services validate the brand function. The product's meaning lies in the promise it fulfils. This forms the content of the buying behaviour policy.

Organisational Expression
An organisation expresses the added value it delivers, especially in the long term. This provides the content for loyalty-building strategic programs.

Only the Message Can Overcome Obstacles

It's crucial to understand that only the message itself has the power to bridge barriers. The method of transmission or the medium used are secondary. Yet, surprisingly, many organisations prioritise the means of communication over the message content.

Too often, companies fixate on creativity. While creativity can enhance message delivery, it's merely a vehicle for the content.

The message's substance remains paramount. Overemphasis on creativity can lead to campaigns remembered for their ingenuity rather than their message or results. Creativity's true role is to illuminate the message, not overshadow it.

Similarly, organisations frequently overvalue the medium. They treat the choice of platform as more critical than the message it carries. However, a medium can only transmit a message; it cannot overcome barriers on its own. The medium's job is simply to deliver the message to the target audience. When selecting a medium, the primary consideration should be its ability to reach your intended recipients effectively.

Always remember: the real success factor lies within the message itself. While organisations employ various forms of expression to convey their messages, ironically, the core message is often left unexpressed. In essence, focus on crafting a powerful, clear message. Let creativity and medium or channel choice serve that message, not overshadow it. Your message is your most potent tool for overcoming obstacles and reaching your audience.

7

Create the correct market proposition

The proposition is your offer to your target group. Without an offer, it's difficult to create brand preference, product buying behaviour, and organisational loyalty. You must give people a reason to choose you, buy from you, and stay with you. To find the most essential and unusual propositions, use the Bitsing method's scorecard analysis. This assesses your entire organisation on market success factors, not just factors you think are important.

Bitsing's Scorecard Analysis

The Bitsing Scorecard Analysis is a powerful tool to assess your organisation's market success factors and discover your uncopyable advantage. This process, which typically takes less than 3 hours, can reveal insights that others might take years to uncover. The analysis consists of 10 steps:

(1)

Step 1: Market pillar analysis

Begin by listing about 60 factors that determine success in your market. Ask yourself: 'If I were to start a competitive organisation tomorrow, what should I excel in?' Include both the factors you're good at and those you're not, as long as they affect market success.

These factors, which we call 'market pillars', support both the market and the organisations within it. They apply to organisations of all sizes and types, from large corporations to non-profits, small businesses to commercial enterprises.

(2)

Step 2: Score yourself

Rate your entire organisation against each market pillar on a scale of 0 to 10. Be objective and factual. A score of 10 means 'excellent', while 0 means 'extremely poor' or 'not applicable'. This step reveals your strengths and weaknesses across all market pillars.

(**3**)

Step 3: Score the competition

Next, score your competitors using the same scale. Consider three types of competitors:

Money competitor

The alternative ways your
target audience could spend their money

Internal competitor

Your own organisation's limitations

Physical competitor

Direct competitors in your market

This step might be challenging, especially regarding the money competitor, but make the best estimates you can.

(**4**)

Step 4: Spot the differences

Compare your scores with those of your competitors. This comparison will highlight which market pillars have the most potential for your organisation.

Step 5: Categorize the market pillars

Divide the market pillars into three categories:

Emotional

These affect feelings and can't be measured.
They relate to brand and preference.

Rational

These are measurable and relate to product
or service features. They influence buying behaviour.

Relational

These form the foundation of loyalty
and connect multiple aspects.

Judge each pillar from your sector's perspective. For example,
an aircraft maintenance company might view 'history' as an
emotional pillar rather than a rational one.

(6)

Step 6: Select the propositions

Choose market pillars where you scored at least two points
higher than your competitors. These will form your propositions:

Emotional pillars become preference propositions

Rational pillars become buying behaviour propositions

Relational pillars become loyalty propositions

Use these propositions in your market development programs. Pillars where you score lower than competitors by two or more points should be subjects for internal improvement.

8

Be uncopyable

I can't stress this enough: if you're copyable you won't be attractive, or be able to overcome barriers. And it won't make achieving your turnover target any easier. Let me illustrate this with a simple yet powerful example.

Example — A tale of two identical parrots

Imagine two identical parrots. They look and sound the same. If I asked you to choose one, which would it be? Time's up!

You've been comparing them, haven't you? And the comparison creates doubt. Why? Because they're so similar - essentially copies of each other. Copyable. So what becomes the deciding factor? On the next page, I guarantee you'll choose the top parrot. Why? Because it's cheaper. When everything else is the same, price prevails.

This is exactly what happens when organisations say and do the same things. They become copyable and therefore comparable. The lesson? When you mirror others, price becomes the only differentiator.

€ 5

€ 15

Uncopyability is thus the key factor, in everything you say and do. Those who rely solely on price or outspending competitors are admitting they're not really different - they're copyable.

Now I have a soft spot for parrots. They're excellent listeners, after all! So I helped our left-hand parrot – who just lost out to his cheaper counterpart – to find his 'uncopyability factor'. I also taught him to communicate his uncopyability effectively. Because if you don't communicate, nothing happens. The result? Our left-hand parrot now advertises his unique ability, which is that he lays golden eggs!

The psychological effect is immediate. This parrot has been laying golden eggs for years, but never realised how special this was. It's something the other parrot can't do and never will. It's truly uncopyable. Suddenly, that 15 euro price tag doesn't seem expensive at all. In fact, it looks like a bargain price for a golden egg-laying parrot!

This is the power of communicating your organisation's 'golden egg' - your uncopyability factor - to your target audience. Price ceases to be an obstacle. Even if competitors outspend you on advertising, they can't replicate your unique value.

We now move on to the next steps of the Scorecard Analysis to uncover your uncopyability.

(**7**)

Step 7: Selecting Potentially Uncopyable Propositions

From your high-scoring propositions, select those with the largest gap between your score and your competitors' scores. These have the potential to be your uncopyable factors.

(8)

Step 8: Broad Uncopyability Selection

Group your selected propositions into sets of 3 or 4. Rank each group from 'hardest to copy' to 'easiest to copy'. This process helps identify your most difficult-to-copy market pillars.

(9)

Step 9: Specific Uncopyability Selection

Repeat the ranking process with the top-ranking pillars from step 8. You're likely to end up with 2 to 3 pillars at the top of your uncopyable selection. You'll often be left with one emotional and one rational pillar. While it might be tempting to choose the rational pillar as your uncopyable factor (especially for those focused on short-term results), the emotional pillar is usually the truly uncopyable element.

(10)

Step 10: Find the 'golden egg'

In this final step, you'll describe the factual evidence of your uncopyability - your 'golden egg'. This is the proof of why your top emotional pillar is truly uncopyable. For example, an aircraft maintenance company discovered that their history of building aircraft was their uncopyable factor. While their competitors only maintained planes, they had been building them for over a century.

The power of uncopyability

Being unique or distinctive isn't enough in today's market. What's truly valuable is being uncopyable. Here's why:

1 **Uniqueness is temporary:** Today's unique selling point can be tomorrow's industry standard.

2 **Price becomes the decider:** When products or services are copyable, customers often choose based on price alone.

3 **True differentiation:** Your uncopyable factor sets you apart in a way competitors can't replicate.

4 **Emotional connection:** The most powerful uncopyable factors are emotional, not rational.

5 **Market dominance:** With a strong uncopyable factor, you can 'own' your market regardless of competitors' actions.

Communicating Your Golden Egg

Once you've identified your golden egg, it's crucial to communicate it effectively:

1 **Make it central to your messaging:** Your uncopyable factor should be at the core of all your communication.

2 **Translate it into customer benefits:** Show how your uncopyable factor benefits your customers.

3 **Use it to justify your value:** A strong uncopyable factor can justify premium pricing.

4 **Embed it in your culture:** Ensure your entire organisation understands and embodies your uncopyable factor.

Conclusion

The Bitsing scorecard analysis is a powerful tool for discovering what truly sets your organisation apart. By finding and leveraging your 'golden egg' you can create a strong, uncopyable market position that drives sustainable success.

Remember, everyone has a golden egg - the key is discovering and communicating it effectively. With your uncopyable factor, you'll be able to overcome market barriers, stand out from competitors and achieve your business goals. You have the 'golden egg'. It makes you uncopyable. It's your uncopyability factor. And that's priceless.

Follow the 10 steps of the scorecard analysis to discover your uncopyable factor:

1
Market pillar analysis
List the factors that determine success in your market. Think broadly and inclusively.

2
Score yourself
Rate your organisation on each factor from 0-10. Be honest and objective.

3
Score the competition
Assess your financial, physical and internal competitors on the same scale.

4
Identify differences
Compare your scores with those of competitors. Note where you differ significantly.

5
Categorise pillars
Divide factors into emotional, rational, and relational. Judge from the perspective of your market sector.

6
Select propositions
Choose factors on which you score at least 2 points higher than competitors. These form your propositions.

---

(7) Select potentially uncopyable factors
Focus on factors with the largest, positive differences
compared to competitors.

(8) Broad uncopyability selection
Group factors and rank them from hardest to easiest to copy.

(9) Specific uncopyability selection
Repeat step 8 with the top factors. You'll end up
with 2-3 hardest-to-copy factors.

(10) Find your 'golden egg'
Deeply investigate the top emotional factor.
Look for the recurring theme that makes you unique.
This is your uncopyable 'golden egg'.

Remember:

Your uncopyable factor, your golden egg, is always emotional

Clearly communicate your golden egg to your target audience

Your golden egg will make you unbeatable in your market

This analysis will enable you to discover, in just a few hours,
what others can struggle with for years. Use your golden egg to
dominate your market, regardless of what competitors do.

Being 'Unbeatable'

The 'golden egg' makes you uncopyable and will be the central
theme in all of your communication. It renders your propositions
credible and is the ultimate proof that your proposition is true.
You now know what policies you need in order to generate brand
preference, product/service purchasing behaviour, and loyalty
in your markets and target groups. You know which propositions to
use in the battle to overcome all three barriers in your target market.

A new supermarket in Europe, without physical stores, only offered home delivery. It was, however, struggling against established market leaders with physical stores. It was on the brink of collapse due to the aggressive sales tactics of these competitors, who could also deliver groceries to homes. The new supermarket seemed to have no competitive advantage. Or so it appeared. That was, until they embraced the Bitsing method and conducted a scorecard analysis.

The results were surprising: the supermarket was uncopyable in the 'real estate' factor. Real estate? You might wonder what that has to do with anything. When asked why they were uncopyable in real estate, they replied, 'We're the only supermarket without expensive, physical stores'.

The established competitors couldn't simply dispose of their brick-and-mortar locations. So this was the new supermarket's uncopyable advantage. They translated this insight into a positioning slogan: 'Supermarket on Wheels.' Moreover, they could legitimately claim to be cheaper, as they didn't bear the costs of expensive, physical storefronts. They could also assert that their products were significantly fresher, since they didn't need to sit on store shelves. The result? Their revenue grew by more than 200%.

This case illustrates how finding your uncopyable factor – even in unexpected areas, like 'real estate' for a delivery-only supermarket – can transform your market position and drive substantial growth. It's not about being unique in obvious ways, but about identifying and leveraging the aspects of your business model that competitors simply cannot replicate.

The following key learnings form the foundation for becoming truly unbeatable in your market, by focusing on what makes you uniquely valuable to your customers.

1 Unbeatability: You are already unbeatable; you just need to discover why. **2** Three Barriers: Always focus on overcoming the Preference, Buying Behaviour and Loyalty barriers.

3 Barrier Focus Strategy: Develop strategies to address all three barriers simultaneously.

4 Policy Development: Create separate policies for Preference, Buying Behaviour and Loyalty. **5** Real Competition: Your true competitor isn't always who you think it is. Find your 'money competitor'. **6** Content Alignment: Use the right content for the right policy – emotional for preference, rational for buying behaviour and relational for loyalty. **7** Market Proposition: Develop propositions that address your target group's needs and decision criteria.

8 Uncopyability: Find your 'golden egg' - the unique, uncopyable factor that sets you apart from competitors. **9** Scorecard Analysis: Use the 10-step Bitsing Scorecard Analysis to identify your market pillars and uncover your uncopyable factor. **10** Message Primacy: The message itself is what overcomes barriers, not creativity or medium choice. **11** Communicating Value: Once you've found your uncopyable factor, effectively communicate it to make price less of an issue for your target audience.

KEY TRAPS TO AVOID

Avoiding these pitfalls can help organisations maintain continuity and achieve sustainable growth, by focusing on what truly makes them unbeatable in their market.

1 **Focusing on internal problems instead of market barriers:** organisations often prioritise solving their own issues rather than addressing customer obstacles.

2 **Neglecting one or more of the three barriers:** concentrating only on buying behaviour while ignoring preference and loyalty can lead to missed opportunities.

3 **Misidentifying competitors:** failing to recognize the 'money competitor' and focusing solely on direct industry competitors can limit growth potential.

4 **Over-reliance on creativity or medium choice:** prioritising how a message is delivered over the content of the message itself can reduce effectiveness.

5 **Trying to be unique instead of uncopyable:** pursuing uniqueness, which can easily be replicated by competitors, rather than finding a truly uncopyable factor.

6 **Failing to communicate the uncopyable factor:** having a 'golden egg', but not effectively sharing it with the target audience.

7 **Competing primarily on price:** when organisations appear similar, price becomes the deciding factor, which can lead to unsustainable competition.

8 **Misaligning content with policy:** using emotional content to drive buying behaviour, or rational content to drive preference, can reduce message effectiveness.

9 **Neglecting to develop separate strategies for preference, buying behaviour and loyalty:** a one-size-fits-all approach can fail to address specific barriers.

10 **Ignoring low-scoring market pillars:** failing to improve areas in which competitors score significantly higher can create vulnerabilities.

11 **Choosing rational factors over emotional ones as the uncopyable element:** the truly uncopyable factor is often emotional rather than rational.

12 **Not conducting a thorough scorecard analysis:** skipping this process can result in missing crucial insights about the organisation's position in the market.

TREAT PEOPLE UNEQUALLY,

BECAUSE NO ONE IS, THINKS, OR BEHAVES THE SAME

MAKE THE MOST OF EVERY PERSON IN YOUR TARGET GROUP

You now know your continuity turnover target (chapter 1) and the choices you must make to reach your goal (chapter 2). You've also established your brand, product, and organisational strategy, you've identified the propositions that will impact your target group, and you've discovered your 'golden egg'. As a result, you're unbeatable and can uninterruptedly pursue and achieve your turnover goal (chapter 3).

Now it's time to convert all of this into action. For unless we take action, nothing will happen. This chapter focuses on the preparatory work for all the activities of your organisation. We will clarify what you need to do to convince all of the people who are necessary for the achievement of your continuity goal.

Forget the Masses

To achieve your turnover objective, you need people. They all belong to target groups. However, a target group member won't necessarily do what you ask. You've probably experienced this: you make a fantastic offer, but only a few people respond. This is because of the assumption that everyone in a target group will be interested in the same offer – i.e. that everyone is the same. If only that were true!

Unfortunately, we're not all interested in the same things, and we certainly aren't the same.

Only a tiny minority is receptive to what you have to say. Don't expect everyone in your target group to cheer when you make your approach. What matters is that you sensitise each individual to your message. An individual approach is the only effective way. Every person is different, with their own thoughts and opinions, and therefore needs to be approached uniquely.

So Many People!

If your target group consists of a million people, trying to approach them in a million different ways is, of course, tricky. Even with twenty, it's complex. But you don't have to do this. We have the BITSER model – which has a very unusual characteristic. It has been shown that every person climbs six steps of a stairway before reaching your goal. If you want to reach every person in a target group individually and help them ascend these six steps, you only need to do six things, regardless of the size of your target audience. To clarify this, I'll take you once more through the BITSER model and let you experience the logic behind the fact that you should always approach a target group via six activities, and that your organisation should be concerned with only these six activities. For a more detailed description of the model, I refer you to the chapter entitled 'The Discovery'.

The BITSER Model

The BITSER model has six steps, which I call the steps of the BITSER stairway (the BITSER funnel, so to speak). Everyone eventually takes these steps to reach your ultimate goal - your continuity turnover target that ensures your company's lasting success. Everything you do should focus on these six steps.

Most organisations unconsciously focus on just one step when approaching their target groups - and often the wrong one. This gives a poor result, which is logical when you see that just one small group has been helped to take one step further, while all others do nothing.

The steps were named in accordance with the barriers that people encounter while taking them. They're grouped here, together with the profiles of the people linked to each step of the BITSER stairway. When you know what kind of personality you're dealing with, it's easier to work with them and obtain a successful result more quickly.

The BITSER Stairway

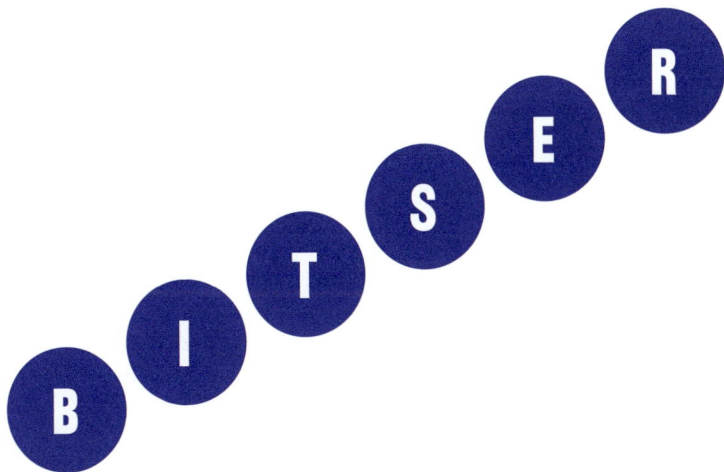

At the Bottom of the Stairway

Here we find the people who are not yet on the first step of the BITSER stairway. They fall within the target group description but are unfamiliar with your brand and organisation's name.

B

Step 1: Brand Awareness – The Potentials

'B' is for 'Brand Awareness'. Without being known, you cannot expect to be recognised or achieve your goals. These are people who have heard about your brand, but haven't yet considered it. They are called Potentials or 'the B's'.

I

Step 2: Image – The Preferrers

'I' stands for 'Image' or 'I want you'. Someone must first desire your brand before they buy, and that's where image comes in.

The people on this step prefer your brand, but aren't ready for action. They are called Preferrers or 'the I's'.

T

Step 3: Traffic - The Movers
'T' stands for 'Traffic'. This involves a visit to the sales location, or an appointment. Without this, people won't take the necessary action, like buying. This is the third BITSER profile. The Movers or 'the T's' are found here. They visited the sales location, but didn't purchase your product or service. They are perhaps not sufficiently convinced to make a purchase.

S

Step 4: Sale - The Buyers
'S' stands for 'Sale'. This can be a transaction, the signing of an employment contract, a staff member's performance, or a behaviour change. Buyers, or 'the S's', are on this fourth step. They've bought the product or service once, but didn't follow up with further, desired behaviour.

E

Step 5: Extra Sales - The Users
'E' is for 'Extra Sales'. This includes repeat orders, multiple product purchases, or continued performance according to your goals and expectations. Users or 'the E's' (Existing customers), are found in this fifth profile. Their interaction with your organisation extends beyond the initial purchase. Ensure that these people extensively use everything your organisation offers, to move them to the next, final step.

R

Step 6: Referral Sales - The Sellers

'R' stands for 'Referral Sales'. These are existing customers who successfully sell your product or service to others, without your intervention. They are Sellers, your true ambassadors, and your most valuable target group. If every customer were a Seller, you wouldn't need to put effort into influencing preference, buying behaviour, or loyalty.

This BITSER stairway model provides a comprehensive framework for understanding and engaging your target audience at every stage of the journey they take with your brand.

As you see, the BITSER model consists of six personal profiles. Your target group, or however else you describe it, consists of these six, personal profiles, and all of them have to climb the same six BITSER steps. You help them do this by directing six activities at your target group.

	BITSER step	Target group
B	Brand Awareness	Potentials
I	Image	Preferrers
T	Traffic	Movers
S	Sale	Buyers
E	Extra Sales	Users
R	Referral Sales	Sellers

Core Elements of Other Target Groups

In the previous section I outlined the personal profiles belonging to each step of the BITSER stairway. These determine how you approach each target group, for example to recruit new customers or to retain existing ones. The profiles for target groups in other 'markets', for instance Human Resources, are the same, but what you want to achieve with them is slightly different.

For example, what you ask of someone whom you want to recruit as a customer differs from what you ask of a potential new staff member. You want the former to purchase a product, while the latter should sign an employment contract. Similarly, expectations regarding improving someone's car-driving behaviour differ from what is expected when asking them to vote for you in an election.

Below is a short description of the core elements of common BITSER model personal profiles for:

1	Personnel recruitment
2	Increasing internal motivation and staff performance
3	Behavioural change
4	Political voting

Regardless of the target group's complexity, the six BITSER steps and seven personal profiles remain the same and are applicable to a broad spectrum.

This scheme provides detailed descriptions of the profile for each of the four categories mentioned above, which I've summarized in a table for clarity and conciseness.

BITSER STEP	PERSONNEL RECRUITMENT	INTERNAL MOTIVATION	BEHAVIOURAL CHANGE	VOTING
SUSPECTS	Never heard of employer's name	Don't know what organisation stands for	Haven't heard of institution	Never heard of political party
B POTENTIALS	Know name, not considering	Understand employer, but don't have a good feeling	Know name, not considering	Heard of party, but not considering
I PREFERRERS	Considering employer, no interview	Feel good, but don't work	Considering institution, no action	Considering party, but don't vote
T MOVERS	Applied, but no employment contract	Work, but don't perform	Trying to change, but unsuccessful	Go to voting station, but don't vote
S BUYERS	Signed, but don't perform	Perform, but minimally	Changed behaviour, but inconsistent	Voted once, but won't again
E USERS	Perform; don't recruit new employees	Perform well; don't motivate colleagues to perform	Consistent, but don't encourage others	Always vote for the party; don't recruit others
R SELLERS	Successfully recruit new employees	Get colleagues to perform	Encourage others	Recruit new voters

I used the BITSER model and its personal profiles in a project for an international company which, according to international norms, values and regulations, could under no circumstances supply to terrorist states. A compliance program was developed, in which thousands of employees were individually addressed to comply with the 'norms, values, and regulations'. And it succeeded! The BITSER stairway personal profiles are always applicable, regardless of the target group, and in any situation. The six activities to help people climb the steps of the stairway are also always applicable. I will tell you about these next.

Help Everyone to Climb the Steps of the BITSER Stairway

Only six things are necessary for this. No more. I call them activities. You will undertake six activities, no more and no less. Just think of the efficiency! Conduct these activities in the best possible way and you will achieve results that others can only dream about - with less effort, less time and less money.

Six Activities That Will Attract Everyone You Need

Each of the six BITSER activities ensures that people on the steps of the BITSER stairway progress to the next step. If you conduct these activities consistently – and don't limit yourself to doing it only once – each person in your target group will climb your BITSER stairway, step by step, and you will grow. It simply cannot go wrong.

Imagine succeeding in growth that's not measured by a few percentage points, but by up to three hundred percent, like many other organisations that have embraced the Bitsing method! And then doing that again, and again. The question isn't whether you'll grow, but whether you can handle that much growth.

Be Proactive

Climbing a stairway can require effort and be quite tiring. Each step is a threshold. That's why you need to see each of the six steps of the BITSER stairway as a difficult-to-overcome obstacle.

People need assistance. The steps won't be taken without a fight and, certainly in the commercial world, nobody will ascend your stairway voluntarily. If you make it easy for people in your target group to take the steps, you'll reach your goals faster. You'll achieve this with a BITSER activity plan. The plan contains an activity relating to each of the six BITSER steps.

The BITSER Model Activities:

B Aims to make your brand known to the target group

I Focuses on creating desire for your brand within the target group

T Drives visits to sales locations or appointments

S Stimulates buying behaviour

E Encourages customer retention and repeat purchases

R Motivates customers to become brand ambassadors

I'll now guide you on how to identify and implement these activities, using the BITSER model in your organisation. This process begins with...

A Bit of Awareness

It's impossible for someone at the bottom of the BITSER stairway to reach the top in a single, large step. You need to help every person in your target audience move upwards, step by step, one at a time. This is where organisations often go wrong. They often only do one thing - and often it's the wrong thing to do. Is it sensible to target someone with an activity relative to a step they've already taken? Offering someone a product they've already bought is neither effective nor efficient.

There's huge wastage in organisations, when it comes to investments made in approaching target groups.

A BITSER Activity Plan - In Three Steps

Drafting a thorough BITSER activity plan isn't complicated. These are the required steps:

1	Choose the target audience.
2	Divide the target group members across the steps of the BITSER stairway.
3	Translate the results into a BITSER activity plan with identified priorities.

I'll now elaborate on each of these steps, providing advice on how to choose the target group, segment it across the steps of the BITSER stairway, and conduct a BITSER ranking analysis.

Creating a BITSER Ranking: A Step-by-Step Guide

1

Choose your target group

Begin with your 'money audience' - the group most likely to generate immediate revenue. The key is focus, focus – and more focus (refer to chapter 2). Other target audiences can be addressed later. I've frequently observed companies achieving their annual turnover goals within ten months, by concentrating on the right target audience and implementing a well-structured BITSER activity plan.

2

Distribute the target group across the steps of the BITSER stairway

People rarely act on their own initiative. They often require an external stimulus – an action or communication undertaken by your organisation, or a direction from a superior. While not everyone is prone to taking initiative it's crucial to recognize this fact, so you can address it. You must provide the right incentives for people in your target market to move forward, especially when you want something from them. To maximise results, it's important to understand which BITSER steps contain the majority of your target group and which contain fewer people. In other words, identify which steps present the biggest obstacles. This knowledge allows you to respond appropriately, set priorities, and focus on the steps that need the most attention. The tool for this analysis is the BITSER ranking.

3

Conduct a BITSER ranking analysis

Regardless of who they are or where they're located, each person's journey follows the six steps of the BITSER stairway. However, the distribution of people across these steps varies between target groups. Understanding this distribution is critical. For example, if there's no one on the third step of the BITSER stairway, how many can proceed to step four? Zero! This is the crux of the matter. If too few or no people are found on any step, there will be few or none who can climb to the next steps.

Consequently, you won't achieve your goal, regardless of your efforts or sacrifices (such as reducing your margin). Conversely, if there are enough people on each step, you're more likely to reach your goal. We'll examine the numerical aspects of this in chapter 6, where I share the secret to predicting your results in advance. To determine how people in your target group(s) are spread across the six steps and which steps form obstacles, you need to perform a BITSER ranking. You'll need a separate ranking for each target group. The six questions described in chapter 3 are useful for this process. Don't worry about perfect rankings at this stage; I'll explain how to verify your BITSER ranking in chapter 6.

Example   BITSER ranking for Jamie Oliver's Restaurant

	Obstacle ranking	Obstacle
B	6	Insufficient brand awareness
I	5	Brand is not considered
T	3	Visits to sale location or appointments are too infrequent
S	2	Visitors to the sales location don't buy
E	4	Existing customers don't continue to buy or they leave
R	1	Existing customers don't recommend the brand to their contacts

In this example, awareness of the restaurant name is the smallest obstacle (B=6), while customers not spontaneously recommending the brand is the largest obstacle (R=1). By following this guide, you can create an effective BITSER ranking to inform your marketing strategy and drive business growth.

Make your own BITSER ranking:

How to Avoid Incorrect BITSER Rankings

When creating a ranking, don't do it from the point of view of your own problem situation. It often happens that, when sales are down, an organisation reacts by giving the sales step the highest rank – this being the problem they want to quickly solve. This is wrong and will lead to the wrong action being taken. A step only justifies a high rank once the people on it do not take action. In other words, the Sales step only justifies a higher rank when those on the Traffic step don't convert to buying.

If people are not buying, it may not necessarily indicate a sales problem. The issue could lie elsewhere in the BITSER model:

Traffic (T) obstacle

Too few people might be visiting the store or scheduling appointments.

Image (I) obstacle

People may not prefer your brand.

Brand awareness (B) obstacle

People might not even know your brand name.

Each of these scenarios represents a different step on the BITSER stairway and requires a unique approach to address. It's crucial to accurately identify where the true obstacle lies in order to implement the most effective solution. By following these principles and using the BITSER model effectively, you can maximise the potential of every person in your target group, leading to significant and sustainable growth for your organisation.

BITSER Ranking for Special Target Groups

When dealing with special target groups, such as in personnel recruitment or behavioural change, adapt the questions using core elements as described in the 'core elements of other target groups' section. You can create a BITSER ranking for diverse groups of people. For instance:

1   **Preparing for a presentation:**
Rank your audience to focus your presentation on the most relevant steps.

2   **Attracting a potential customer:**
Determine which step they're on in order to tailor your approach.

3   **Job interviews:**
Create a BITSER ranking of the interviewers to increase your chances of success.

4   **Facing redundancy:**
Rank those who decide your fate in order to better handle the situation.

Regardless of the parties you're dealing with, BITSER ranking can help you identify which obstacles (BITSER steps) to focus on.

The Forgotten Target Group: Influencers

Don't overlook influencers. While they don't directly generate financial gain, they influence those who do. Your 'paying public' is affected by people in their environment, such as colleagues or family. Create a BITSER ranking for these influencers too, but the paying customer should remain your primary focus.

The Whole Organisation

Everyone in your organisation is already ascending one of the six BITSER steps, consciously or unconsciously. You can distribute your entire organisation across these steps. Everything revolves around them. The BITSER stairway is your organisation and is essential for your success.

Results Translated into a BITSER Activity Plan, with Priorities

The BITSER ranking numbers indicate each step's contribution to the obstacles hindering your continuity goal achievement.

Step 1 presents the biggest obstacle, step 6 the smallest. Steps 1, 2, and 3 constitute the majority of problems. They pose the biggest risks to achieving your turnover target and demand top priority, direct action and significant attention. Steps 4, 5, and 6 complete the system. They're less problematic but help extract more from your target group to achieve your continuity turnover goal.

An Internal BITSER Plan is Essential

An internal plan based on the Bitsing method is crucial for staff. Employees are responsible for everything that happens in the organisation. They must also climb six BITSER steps to optimise their contribution to achieving objectives. A well-functioning internal organisation means the battle for success is already half won.

Describing and Prioritising the Obstacle

After analysing the ranking, draw conclusions and draft an action plan. The first part provides insight into the obstacles and the order of priority of the BITSER steps:

B Insufficient brand awareness.

I Brand not considered.

T Too little or no visits to sale location; or no appointments.

S Visitors to the sales location don't buy.

E Existing customers are not retained; do not carry on buying.

R Existing customers are unsuccessful in selling you to their contacts.

The Activity Mix

The six BITSER steps require six activities:

B Establish brand awareness among those who don't know the brand name.

I Communicate brand image to those who do not consider the brand.

T Achieve traffic in sales locations among those who do not visit the sales location.

S Stimulate sales among those not buying the product or service.

E Extra sales stimulation for those who don't continue to buy all your organisation has to offer.

R Promote referral sales – to activate those who do not sell to their contacts.

These activities, in turn, guide the specific actions required to assist people to advance to the next step.

A BITSER activity plan consists of a mix of activities, each with its own priorities, aimed at the corresponding personal profile. Identify which three activities have the highest priority and which have lower priority. Also, determine which personal profile you'll encounter most and which will present the fewest problems. Targeting someone with the wrong activity is ineffective. Select high-priority activities that fit the relevant personal profile to ensure you address the right issues and succeed.

Formulate the Appropriate Barrier Focus Strategy

In chapter 3, I briefly introduced the barrier strategy. You always need to overcome three barriers: the preference barrier (focusing on your brand), the buying behaviour barrier (focusing on your product or service), and the loyalty barrier (focusing on your internal organisation).

At this point, you don't know which of these barriers requires the most emphasis. You'll want to discover the extent to which each barrier plays a role in your markets and target groups and, consequently, how much focus each requires. By the end of this section, the answer to these questions will be clear. You'll discover which focus percentage to apply to each barrier using the BITSER model, deriving three percentages that indicate the attention needed to overcome each barrier. This variable degree of focus is called the barrier focus strategy.

The BITSER Model and the Barriers

Use the six steps of the BITSER model to detect the three focus percentages relative to the barriers:

B + I: Lead to brand preference

T + S: Lead to product/service purchase behaviour

E + R: Lead to customer loyalty towards the internal organisation

The Barrier Focus Percentages

You must pay attention to each barrier, but how much? Express this as a percentage. Knowing the percentage of attention a barrier requires allows you to formulate internal and external strategies more easily. Use the BITSER model to establish these percentages by creating a BITSER ranking.

Allocate a score reflecting the dominance of each step to create a BITSER ranking, as you learned in the previous pages. Rank 1 is the biggest obstacle, rank 6 the smallest.

Example | BITSER ranking for The National Ballet

The BITSER ranking for The National Ballet can be seen in the table below:

B	I	T	S	E	R
4	1	6	3	2	5

Converting BITSER Rankings to Focus Percentages

To translate BITSER rankings into actionable insights, convert them to percentages. This process reveals the relative importance of each step:

1 Add up the six ranking numbers (total 21).

2 Divide each ranking number by 21 and multiply by 100.

3 Round up the results for simplicity.

The rounded percentages are:

Rank 1 = 30% focus

Rank 2 = 25% focus

Rank 3 = 20% focus

Rank 4 = 15% focus

Rank 5 = 10% focus

Rank 6 = 5% focus

The highest focus is 30%, the lowest is 5%, and each step differs by 5%. This simple pattern makes the percentages easy to remember and apply. The total slightly exceeds 100% due to rounding, but this doesn't affect the model's effectiveness.

These percentages indicate where to allocate your resources and efforts in your BITSER strategy to ensure a balanced, yet prioritised, approach to your target audience.

	BITSER level rank	The National Ballet focus	My ranking	My BITSER focus
B	4	15%	....	.... %
I	1	30%	....	.... %
T	6	5%	....	.... %
S	3	20%	....	.... %
E	2	25%	....	.... %
R	5	10%	....	.... %

B + I: Form the preference barrier

T + S: Constitute the buying behaviour barrier

E + R: Form the loyalty barrier

Add up the percentages for each barrier to determine the focus percentage for each:

B + I: 15%+30% = 45% brand preference focus

T + S: 5%+20% = 25% product buying focus

E + R: 25%+10% = 35% organisation loyalty focus

These three forms of policy are interconnected and drive each other, like gears. If the preference gear doesn't turn, there's no movement in buying behaviour or loyalty.

Gear 1 = 45% brand preference focus

Gear 2 = 25% product buying focus

Gear 3 = 35% organisation loyalty focus

Due to rounding up, the total of the percentages is 105%.

This gives you a clear picture of which barriers need the most attention in your strategy. You can now establish a focus strategy for every continent, country, region, market, sector and target group.

A Tip!

Everything changes after you've engaged a target group. Nothing stays the same – because you are, after all, actively working to eradicate the obstacles. A BITSER ranking will therefore also change over time. Periodic analysis using BITSER ranking is important, to see whether an activity plan still applies to the actual problems that prevail in a target group. Make adjustments if the ranking changes.

The Power of Consistent Communication

The classical approach to target groups is often suboptimal. However, this presents an opportunity: by adopting a more effective method, you could potentially improve performance by up to 300%! Traditional marketing often relies on repetitive campaigns that fail to address all steps of the BITSER stairway, limiting the potential reach within a target group. Moreover, communication typically ceases between campaigns, leading to periods of silence during which goals remain unachieved.

	WEEK	NEW CUSTOMERS YEAR OF CONVENTIONAL MARKETING	NEW CUSTOMERS YEAR OF BITSING (GREY)	DIFFERENCE IN RESULTS (BITSING = GREY)
JUNE	23	38	30	-8
	24	31	28	-3
	25	34	36	+2
	26	20	30	+10
JULY	27	19	31	+12
	28	16	22	+6
	29	22	18	-4
	30	18	28	+10
AUGUST	31	19	22	+3
	32	13	20	+7
	33	25	35	+10
	34	27	51	+24
	35	27	38	+11
SEPTEMBER	36	27	57	+30
	37	33	48	+15
	38	18	27	+9
	39	14	37	+23
OCTOBER	40	18	33	+15
	41	29	37	+8
	42	15	14	-1
	43	19	26	+7
NOVEMBER	44	22	26	+4

The following example demonstrates how communication becomes significantly more effective when based on the six steps of the BITSER model.

Example   An educational institution's recruitment drive

An educational institution needed to recruit students to meet its turnover goal. The study compares two consecutive years:

Year 1)   Conventional marketing approach
Year 2)   Bitsing method applied, with campaigns
            structured according to the BITSER mode

The results:

1
Overall growth:
The Bitsing method year showed higher recruitment numbers compared to the conventional year.

2
Exceptions to growth:
Weeks 23, 24, 29 and 42 showed poorer performance than the previous year.

Analysis of exceptions:

Weeks 23-24	Still used the conventional approach (single repeated campaign)
Weeks 25-28	Implemented six campaigns aligned with BITSER steps, resulting in growth
Week 29	Implemented six campaigns aligned with BITSER steps, resulting in growth
Weeks 30-41	Outstanding results, some weeks showing over 100% growth
Week 42	Another decline as the school paused campaigns during autumn vacation

Key learnings:

---

1 Consistent application of all six BITSER steps
leads to growth.

---

2 Stopping communication, even briefly,
can lead to an immediate decline in results.

---

3 The BITSER model works across various periods and
conditions, provided it's consistently applied.

The Conclusion

Communicate and you will achieve your goal! Consistently apply
the steps of the BITSER model and growth will ensue. And don't
stop to see what happens, you'll stop growing. The key learnings
for this chapter are:

1

Individualised approach:
Treat people in your target group unequally,
recognizing that each person is unique.

2

BITSER model:
Use this six-step model (Brand awareness,
Image, Traffic, Sales, Extra sales, Referral
sales) to structure your approach.

3

Continuous communication:
Maintain consistent communication
across all BITSER steps.

4

Regular ranking:
Perform BITSER rankings regularly to
understand where your obstacles lie.

5

Adaptive strategy:
Adjust your strategy based on the results
of your BITSER rankings.

6

Tailored activities:
Create specific activities for each step
of the BITSER model.

7

Internal focus:
Implement an internal BITSER plan
for your employees.

8

Barrier focus:
Pay attention to all three barriers
(Preference, Buying Behaviour, Loyalty).

9

Influencer consideration:
Include influencers in your strategy, but
don't let them dominate your focus.

10

Step-by-step progression:
Help people climb the BITSER stairway
one step at a time.

11

Holistic view:
Consider your entire organisation in
the context of the BITSER model.

12

Growth potential:
Consistent application of the BITSER model
can lead to significant growth (up to 300%).

13

Proactive approach:
Be proactive in helping your target group
overcome obstacles at each step.

14

Prioritisation:
Focus more resources on the steps that
present the biggest obstacles.

15

Dynamic strategy:
Recognize that your BITSER ranking will change over time as you address obstacles.

16

Measurement:
Continuously measure and analyse the effectiveness of your activities.

17

Cross-functional alignment:
Ensure all parts of your organisation are aligned with your BITSER strategy.

18

Long-term perspective:
Focus on building lasting relationships rather than just immediate sales.

19

Efficiency:
The BITSER model allows for efficient use of resources by focusing on the most impactful activities.

20

Scalability:
The BITSER model can be applied to various target groups and scenarios, from customer acquisition to employee motivation.

THE KEY PITFALLS TO AVOID

By avoiding these pitfalls, a company can develop a more robust and effective strategy that leads to sustainable growth and long-term success.

1 **Mass approach:** the trap of treating your entire target group as one homogeneous mass, instead of recognising that each individual is unique.

2 **One-sided focus:** the danger of concentrating on just one step of the BITSER model, while all six steps require attention.

3 **Subjective ranking:** creating a BITSER ranking based on your perception of your own problem, rather than on the actual situation in your target group.

4 **Inconsistent communication:** stopping communication after a campaign, instead of consistently continuing.

5 **Misaligned activities:** directing an activity at people who have already passed the Bitser step to which that activity relates.

6 **Ignoring internal organisation:** neglecting the internal BITSER strategy in favour of external marketing.

7 **Static strategy:** sticking to an unchanged strategy without regular recalibration of the BITSER ranking.

8 **Underestimating loyalty:** underestimating the importance of the loyalty barrier and the power of existing customers for referrals.

9 **Skipping steps:** trying to get people from the bottom to the top of the BITSER stairway in one go, instead of working step by step.

10 **Ignoring influencers:** overlooking the role of influencers in your target group's decision-making process.

11 **Short-term thinking:** focusing on quick results at the expense of long-term growth and customer relationships.

12 **Overgeneralisation:** applying the same BITSER strategy to all markets or target groups without considering specific differences.

THE LEARNINGS FROM THIS CHAPTER

The Do's

1 Treat people in your target group individually, recognising that everyone is different. **2** Use the BITSER model to structure your approach to different target groups. **3** Consistently apply all six steps of the BITSER model (Brand awareness, Image, Traffic, Sales, Extra sales, Referral sales). **4** Regularly perform BITSER rankings to understand where your obstacles lie. **5** Adapt your strategy based on the results of your BITSER rankings. **6** Create tailored activities for each step of the BITSER model. **7** Consider influencers as a separate target group, but don't let them dominate your focus. **8** Implement an internal BITSER plan for your employees. **9** Maintain continuous communication with your target groups. **10** Regularly recalibrate your BITSER rankings as your target group evolves.

THE LEARNINGS FROM THIS CHAPTER

The Don'ts

1 Don't treat everyone in your target group the same way. **2** Don't focus only on one step of the BITSER model. **3** Don't create a BITSER ranking that's based on your own problem situation rather than the actual situation in your target group. **4** Don't stop to communicate after a campaign ends. **5** Don't ignore the importance of any of the three barriers (Preference, Buying Behaviour, Loyalty). **6** Don't assume that what worked in the past will continue to work, without adjustment. **7** Don't neglect your internal organisation in favour of external marketing. **8** Don't target people using activities related to steps they've already taken. **9** Don't ignore the potential of your existing customers for referral sales. **10** Don't underestimate the power of consistent, ongoing communication in driving growth.

By following the do's and avoiding the don'ts, a company can create a robust, adaptable strategy that addresses the needs of its target groups effectively, leading to sustainable growth and longevity.

A FOCUSED
MESSAGE

GETS A LISTENING AUDIENCE

THIS IS HOW YOU DEPLOY EFFECTIVE PROCESSES AND PROGRAMMES

A fundamental truth in business strategy is this: the primary reason good strategies fail is poor execution. In fact, implementation is so critical that it deserves to be emphasised three times, implementation, implementation – and implementation! Even the best plans can fail due to poor execution.

This chapter will reveal the secrets for successful implementation of your overall Bitsing plan and BITSER activity plan, transforming your strategy into effective actions.

The Power of the Bitsing Plan

A Bitsing plan engages your entire organisation without adding to anyone's workload. It's almost self-completing due to its obviousness and will save time while driving growth. As Sven Kramer from Shell International notes, 'Bitsing remains impressive in its simplicity and accuracy'. The plan focuses on six, clear activities that will ensure organisational continuity. This focus often leads to improvements in effectiveness measured in tens of percent, and savings in time, resources and money of over 25%. Whether you work alone or with thousands of employees, these six activities are the key to the healthy continuation of your organisation.

Always: A Mix of Programme Activities

When implementing a Bitsing plan, you'll never focus on just one, dominant issue. Instead, your organisation will work on six different activities, each engaging with the steps of the BITSER stairway. Each step requires its own activity to help people progress. You'll launch external programmes to entice target groups that are crucial for your continuity turnover goal, and internal programmes aimed at your employees, who will enable achievement of these goals.

Let's now explore the key cornerstones for effectively preparing and implementing these programmes. Following these and you'll be well on your way to achieving your continuity target!

| The six Bitser programmes |
| **B** Establish awareness |
| **I** Create brand preference |
| **T** Generate traffic at point of sale |
| **S** Achieve product sales |
| **E** Stimulate extra sales |
| **R** Stimulate referrals |

1

Cornerstone 1: Implement six targeted programmes

In chapter 4 I dealt extensively with the three types of policies for removing all the barriers that stand in the way of achieving your continuity goal: the preference, buying and loyalty barriers. You execute these policies using the six BITSER programmes.

| B + I: Execute the brand preference policy |
| T + S: Actualise the product or service buying behaviour policy |
| E + R: Implement the organisation loyalty policy |

2

Cornerstone 2: Follow the BITSER programme strategy

Resources are finite: money can only be spent once, while your people, time and attention are capped at 100%. Strategic allocation is key. Allocate attention percentages to each programme based on the BITSER ranking from chapter 4. The ranking indicates a programme's priority; the percentages form the programme strategy.

From BITSER Ranking to Programme Strategy

Calculating programme focus percentages builds on the BITSER ranking method outlined in chapters 3 and 4. As a quick refresher – Conversion of BITSER Ranking to Focus Percentages:

Programme ranking 1 =	30% focus
Programme ranking 2 =	25% focus
Programme ranking 3 =	20% focus
Programme ranking 4 =	15% focus
Programme ranking 5 =	10% focus
Programme ranking 6 =	5% focus
Total capped at:	100% available focus/attention

The total of the percentages is 105% due to rounding.

With this conversion in mind, you can now allocate focus percentages to each programme based on your BITSER ranking. An example:

	Ranking	Focus
B	4	15%
I	1	30%
T	5	10%
S	3	20%
E	2	25%
R	6	5%

Assess Your Organisation: Where Is Your Focus?

Which of these activities consumes more than 40%* of your organisation's resources (energy, time, money and/or personnel)?

- Sales
- Production
- Recruitment
- Marketing
- Product development
- Innovation
- Cost Reduction
- Internal Motivation
- Problem Solving
- Customer Retention
- Other: _____

*Note: 40% is excessive. The Bitsing model recommends a maximum of 30% for optimal effectiveness.

What Does Percentage of Attention Mean?

1 **Dedication**: The programme's share of all activities. No single programme should exceed 30% of all activities, regardless of the challenges you face.

2 **Alertness**: Higher percentages indicate greater importance for success. The higher the percentage, the more critically you should check the programme's content.

3 **Concentration**: Focus on the three highest percentages, which address 75% of obstacles in your market and target audience. Focusing on a single programme is ineffective.

4 **Money**: Use percentages as a guide for budget allocation. For example, if you have 100 euros to spend, allocate 30 euros to the programme with the 30% share.

The Perfection of the Programme Strategy

The percentages indicate the intensity with which you help every person in your target market ascend the BITSER stairway in the fastest way. Pushing too hard or too little doesn't help people progress.

To Each Programme its Own Effect

Each BITSER programme has its own, specific requirements and effects. The S programme, aimed at selling your product does little for awareness, but sells your product. The B programme builds awareness, but doesn't sell.

3

Cornerstone 3: Allocate Tasks To Programmes, Not Objectives

Give someone a task, not a goal, to ensure achievement. Imagine you're parched and need water. You say to your assistant, 'I'd like to wet my throat.' The result? Unpredictable. You might get water, or perhaps a cough drop, or even a humidifier! Now, contrast that with a clear directive, 'Could you please bring me a glass of water?' The outcome? Crystal clear, just like the water you'll receive.

This simple scenario illustrates a fundamental principle of the BITSER activity plan. Each programme in the plan, and by extension every individual involved, is assigned a precise task. These aren't vague objectives, but clear, actionable directives. By transforming nebulous goals into specific tasks, we create a direct path to achievement. It's not about hoping for results, it's about engineering them, with clarity and precision.

Each BITSER programme and its specific task:

B	Attract attention
I	Be irresistible
T	Activate
S	Be convincing
E	Retain customers
R	Bind relationships

4

Cornerstone 4: Always Choose The Right Subject

Each BITSER message revolves around one, distinct subject. This singular focus is not just a suggestion—it's a fundamental principle for maximising effectiveness.

Why is this so crucial? When you dilute your message with multiple topics, you dramatically diminish its impact. You fragment your audience's attention and your key point gets lost in the noise.

Single-Subject Focus in BITSER Programmes

Remember: Every BITSER programme is characterised by its unique, individual subject. This isn't a guideline to follow loosely – it's a rule to embrace wholeheartedly. In the world of the BITSER stairway, less truly is more. By concentrating on one subject per activity, you amplify the power of your message and significantly boost your chances of achieving your goals. So, stay disciplined. Stay focused. One BITSER message; one subject. Your results will speak for themselves.

Each BITSER programme deals with a separate subject:

- **B** Brand or organisation NAME (brand awareness)
- **I** Brand IDENTITY and meaning
- **T** Sales LOCATION or distribution channel
- **S** PRODUCT or service to be bought
- **E** Your organisation's value-added EXTRA Offerings
- **R** Customer RELATIONSHIP

These subjects should be familiar and clearly recognisable to both your organisation (internal programme) and your target audience (external programme). By following these criteria and understanding the role of each programme, you can effectively implement your Bitsing plan and achieve your continuity goals.

5

Cornerstone 5: Don't Talk Nonsense

In organisations, nonsense refers to meaningless words or irrelevant communication. It's easy to fall into the trap of using empty phrases or misaligned messages. Here are some examples of nonsense, as used in (too) many organisations:

1	Calling someone a client when they're not
2	Trying to sell before establishing brand awareness
3	Using sales techniques to build awareness
4	Explaining your brand's value to loyal customers who already know it

These practices result in ineffective communication that fails to resonate with the target audience. To avoid this, each BITSER programme must adhere to its own set of technical criteria. Applying the wrong criteria can be counterproductive, turning a potentially constructive programme into a destructive one.

Basis Techniques of the BITSER Programmes

Let's delve into the core techniques for each BITSER programme to maximise effectiveness and eliminate inefficiencies:

B Programme (establish awareness)

Goal: Make your brand known to the target group.
Key techniques:

1. Capture attention through standout elements
2. Use surprising and memorable approaches
3. Keep campaigns short and impactful
4. Allocate resources based on the programme's focus percentage

I Programme (Create Brand Preference)

Goal: Give weight and significance to your brand.
Key techniques:

1. Utilise emotional propositions (refer to chapter 3)
2. Highlight your brand's unique, uncopyable factor (the 'golden egg')
3. Adopt a dynamic approach to brand activation
4. Evoke emotions to position the brand effectively
5. Project authority without arrogance

T Programme (Generate Traffic)

Goal: Drive the target group to the sales location.
Key techniques:

1 Focus on the sales location or distribution channel

2 Remove barriers to desired behaviour

3 Offer risk-free, non-commercial activities

4 Create unforced, refreshing, external campaigns

5 Lower thresholds to action

S Programme (Achieve Product Sales)

Goal: Convert interest into purchases.
Key techniques:

1 Deploy rational propositions about your product/service (see chapter 3)

2 Force quick purchasing decisions

3 Shorten consideration time

4 Focus on the deal rather than pushing the product

5 Offer value benefits connected to the product/service

4 Use limited-time offers to create urgency

5 Adapt approaches for consumer vs. business markets

E Programme (Stimulate Extra Sales)

Goal: Encourage additional purchases from existing customers. **Key techniques:**

1. Ensure customer satisfaction as a prerequisite

2. Clearly communicate the value of extra purchases

3. Focus on customer retention

4. Offer unconditional rewards to show appreciation. These are rewards that don't require a request or mandatory purchase in return

5. Provide non-commercial, useful benefits

6. Maintain a service-oriented tone in campaigns

R Programme (Stimulate Referrals)

Goal: Build relationships with loyal customers and encourage referrals. **Key techniques:**

1. Foster loyalty through personal connections

2. Utilise relational propositions (refer to chapter 3)

3. Involve client service staff as key players

4. Ask customers to acquire new customers

5. Recognise and appreciate customer relationships

6. Involve customers in your organisation

7. Create lasting personal bonds between customers and staff

Summary

If your BITSER programmes meet their technical criteria, they will do their job effectively.

B programme

Target person profile: Non customer
(to be converted to Potential)

Subject: brand or organisation name

Task: generate attention

Strategy: get noticed

Execution: surprising

Tone-of-voice: short & sharp

I programme

Target person profile: Potential
(to be converted to Preferrer)

Subject: identity of brand or organisation (chapter 3)

Task: become unbeatable

Strategy: be irresistible

Message: emotional propositions (see chapter 3)

Execution: uncopyable benefit (your golden egg)

Tone-of-voice: authoritative

T programme

Target person profile: Preferrer
(to be converted to Mover)

Subject: sales location

Task: activate

Strategy: remove obstacles to action

Execution: risk-free offer

Tone-of-voice: unforced

S programme

Target person profile: Mover
(to be converted to Buyer)

Subject: product or service

Task: force decision

Strategy: a deal

Message: rational propositions (see chapter 3)

Execution: limited time value offer

Tone-of-voice: confrontational (direct)

E programme

Target person profile: Buyer
(to be converted to User)

Subject: all the extras you can offer

Task: retain (bind)

Strategy: appreciate the buyer

Execution: obligation-free reward

Tone-of-voice: service-oriented

R programme

Target person profile: User
(to be converted to Seller)

Subject: relationship

Task: bind

Strategy: recognise the relationship

Message: relational propositions (see chapter 3)

Execution: involve user with the organisation
and increase user/organisation interaction

Tone-of-voice: (doing it) together

Cornerstone 6: Make Sure You Are Seen, Because Seeing Is Believing

Even the best programme is ineffective if it doesn't reach your target group. This applies to both external and internal programmes. The impact and effect of your internal programmes should be visible to your external audience as well.

IT IS POSSIBLE TO HAMMER A SCREW INTO A WALL, BUT YOU'LL GET THE BEST RESULT WITH A SCREWDRIVER.

Your BITSER programme is communicated through various media. Choose media that align with each programme's goals and maximise visibility. For instance, someone who's uninterested in your brand won't engage with a retail promotion featuring your products.

If you adhere to these criteria and techniques, you will create BITSER programmes that communicate effectively, you'll avoid nonsense, and you'll achieve your continuity turnover target:

1	Recognise that each medium has specific strengths
2	Match programmes to the media in which they're most effective
3	Avoid random media selection based on personal preference or financial interests
4	Ensure your chosen media can effectively reach your target audience

BITSER Programmes and Media Requirements

In today's complex media landscape, with over hundred available media types, and more emerging every day, choosing the right medium for your BITSER programmes can be challenging. The key is to focus on media characteristics rather than the medium itself. Each BITSER programme requires specific media traits to effectively help your target audience progress to the next step.

Below is the list of key media characteristics, matched to the programmes they fit best. I call this the media strategy for BITSER Programmes.

B	B media	Inevitable
I	I media	Imaginative
T	T media	Interactive
S	S media	At point of sale
E	E media	Deliverable
R	R media	Entertaining

Learn from the Characteristics of Different Media Types

Characteristics of B media (Inevitable)

1	Impactful and attention-grabbing
2	Broad coverage of target group
3	Difficult to avoid or ignore
4	Resistant to competing stimuli
5	Effective within short periods
6	Mass, unavoidable, fleeting, fast, no noise

Characteristics of I media (Imaginary)

1	Dynamic and emotion-stirring
2	Capable of conveying images and sound
3	Selective and emotive
4	Matched to specific target groups
5	Fits brand personality
6	May have social authority
7	Selectively deployable, dynamic, emotive conveys images/sound

Characteristics of T media (Interactive)

1. Enables direct response
2. Feels personally addressed
3. Reaches precise number of people
4. Activating and engaging
5. Works in personal environment
6. Direct, (re)active, responsive, accessible

Characteristics of S media (On The Spot)

1. Direct and confrontational at sales location
2. Impactful and persuasive
3. Temporary and relevant at point of purchase
4. Present at moment of decision
5. Confrontational, at sales location, temporary, at moment of deal

Characteristics of E media (Deliverable)

1. Service-oriented
2. Personal and appreciative
3. Brings value to the recipient
4. Often generated within the organisation
5. Personal, giving, service-oriented, appreciative

Characteristics of R media (Entertaining)	
1	Connects and binds
2	Focused on individual interaction
3	More like 'live entertainment'
4	Creates neutral, non-commercial environment
5	Strengthens customer relationships
6	Individual, involved, relational, together

People and BITSER Programmes

Matching the right personality to each BITSER programme is crucial for success:

B Demands a standout personality

I Requires an impassioned personality

T Needs a door-opener (not a salesperson)

S Requires an effective closer

E Demands a service-oriented person

R Needs a relationship specialist

Categorising personalities:

B + I: The Missionaries

T + S: The Hunters

E + R: The Farmers

Programme Frequency

Programme frequency refers to how often you approach your target audience during a specified period. It represents the number of times you present an activity from a specific BITSER programme to individuals at each step of the BITSER stairway.

Guidelines for different markets:

Consumer market (B2C)

4 approaches yield 1 real contact

Business market (B2B)

2 approaches yield 1 contact

Internal market (B2E)

1 approach yields 1 contact

Optimal Frequency According to Programme Focus

Based on BITSER Programme Implementation over a three-month period:

B2C		
30% focus:	24x	(2x per week for 3 months)
25% focus:	20x	(3x per 2 weeks)
20% focus:	16x	(1x per 1.5 weeks)
15% focus:	12x	(1x per week)
10% focus:	8x	(1x per 2 weeks)
5% focus:	4x	(1x per 3 weeks)

B2B		
30% focus:	12x	(1x per week for 3 months)
25% focus:	10x	(1x per 1.5 weeks)
20% focus:	8x	(1x per 1.5 weeks)
15% focus:	6x	(1x per 2 weeks)
10% focus:	4x	(1x per 3 weeks)
5% focus:	2x	(1x per 6 weeks)

B2E		
30% focus:	6x	(1x per 2 weeks for 3 months)
25% focus:	5x	(1x per 2.5 weeks)
20% focus:	4x	(1x per 3 weeks)
15% focus:	3x	(1x per 4 weeks)
10% focus:	2x	(1x per 6 weeks)
5% focus:	1x	(1x per 12 weeks)

Programme Strategy: Balancing Frequency and Intensity

The programme strategy dictates both frequency and intensity of implementation. Programmes demanding a high level of attention require greater intensity compared to those needing minimal attention.

Three distinct frequency strategies exist:

1	Introductory
2	Building
3	Maintained

Each strategy aligns with different levels of programme focus (in the above table of focus percentages) and resource allocation.

1 Introductory intensity (the 30% and 25% levels of focus): high frequency, short period

2 Building intensity (20% and 15% focus levels): moderate frequency, medium-length period

3 Maintained intensity (10% and 5% focus): low frequency, long period

The Importance of Timing

Adjust your BITSER activities based on changing circumstances and market conditions. Divide your target period into smaller sub-periods (quarters, months or weeks) for better adaptability. Remember that the time between first contact and final purchase can vary greatly, especially in B2B markets or for complex products/services.

From Theory to Practise

While this book provides valuable insights, becoming an experienced 'Bitser' requires practical application. Start by creating your own effective programmes now and build experience as quickly as possible. Remember, knowledge comes from books, but true expertise comes from practice.

By internalising the following learnings, readers can more effectively implement the BITSER method, avoiding common pitfalls and maximising their chances of success in achieving their organisational goals.

1

Implementation Triad:
Remember, the three main reasons strategies fail are implementation, implementation – and implementation. Execution is crucial.

2

Resource Allocation:
Your resources (time, money, people, attention) are finite. Strategic allocation is the key to success.

3

BITSER Ranking:
Use the BITSER ranking to determine focus percentages for each programme. This ensures balanced attention across all areas.

4

30% Rule:
No single programme should receive more than 30% of your organisation's focus. This maintains balance and prevents neglect of other crucial areas.

5

Task-Oriented Approach:
Assign specific tasks rather than vague objectives. This clarity leads to better execution and results.

6

Single-Subject Focus:
Each BITSER programme should focus on one, distinct subject. This increases the effectiveness of your efforts.

7

Media Matching:
Choose media based on their characteristics and how well they align with each BITSER programme's goals.

8

Personality Fit:
Match the right personalities to each BITSER programme for optimal performance.

9

Frequency and Intensity:
Adjust the frequency and intensity of your programmes based on their focus percentages and your target market.

10

Timing Considerations:
Be mindful of the time between first contact and final purchase when planning your programmes, especially in B2B contexts.

11

Adaptive Planning:
Divide your target period into smaller sub-periods to allow for better adaptability to changing circumstances.

12

Continuous Learning:
Remember that while theory is important,
true expertise comes from practical
application of the BITSER method.

13

Holistic Approach:
Implement all six BITSER programmes
simultaneously to achieve
a comprehensive strategy.

14

Avoid Nonsense:
Ensure all communication is relevant
and aligned with the specific goals
of each BITSER step.

15

Value of Specificity:
Use precise, targeted approaches
for each programme rather than generic,
one-size-fits-all solutions.

PITFALLS THREATENING THE HEALTH AND SURVIVAL OF YOUR BUSINESS

Once you're aware of these pitfalls you can navigate
the implementation of the BITSER method more effectively,
avoiding common mistakes that could undermine success.

1

The implementation trap:
The belief that a good strategy alone is enough.
Remember, implementation is crucial, and poor
implementation is often the reason strategies fail.

2

The single-focus fallacy:
Concentrating more than 40% of resources on
a single activity or programme. This imbalance can
lead to neglect of other crucial areas.

3

The vague objective snare:
Setting general goals instead of specific,
actionable tasks. This can lead to confusion
and ineffective execution.

4

The mismatched media mistake:
Choosing media for programmes based on personal
preference or convenience rather than their suitability
for the specific BITSER step.

5

The one-size-fits-all error:
Applying the same approach to all BITSER
programmes, ignoring their unique characteristics
and requirements.

6   **The short-term vision trap:** Failing to consider the entire customer journey, from first contact to final purchase, when planning programmes.

7   **The overcomplication pitfall:** Trying to address multiple subjects within a single BITSER programme and diluting its effectiveness.

8   **The rigid planning mistake:** Not dividing long-term goals into shorter, adaptable sub-periods, making it difficult to adjust to changing circumstances.

9   **The expertise illusion:** Assuming that understanding the BITSER method theoretically is enough, without recognising the importance of practical application.

10   **The communication confusion:** Mixing messages or using inappropriate techniques for different BITSER steps, leading to ineffective or counterproductive outcomes.

11   **The resource allocation error:** Spreading resources too thinly across all programmes instead of strategic resource allocation based on BITSER ranking.

12   **The personality mismatch trap:** Assigning people to BITSER programmes without considering whether their personality fits the programme's requirements.

THE LEARNINGS FROM THIS CHAPTER

The Do's

1 Implement all six BITSER programmes simultaneously. **2** Follow the programme strategy and allocate attention according to BITSER ranking. **3** Focus on a single subject per programme for maximum effectiveness.
4 Choose media that best match the characteristics of each BITSER programme.
5 Adjust the frequency and intensity of programmes based on their focus percentage.
6 Ensure a good match between personalities and BITSER programmes. **7** Plan programmes considering the time between first contact and final purchase. **8** Use the correct techniques for each, specific BITSER programme.
9 Divide long-term goals into shorter sub-periods for better adaptability. **10** Aim for a maximum focus of 30% per programme.

THE LEARNINGS FROM THIS CHAPTER

The Don'ts

1 Avoid focusing on just one dominant issue or programme. **2** Don't use incorrect techniques for a particular BITSER programme. **3** Don't spend more than 40% of attention on a single activity. **4** Avoid talking nonsense; steer clear of irrelevant communication. **5** Don't set vague goals; set clear, specify tasks. **6** Don't ignore the unique characteristics of different media types. **7** Don't confuse programme objectives with programme tasks. **8** Don't underestimate the importance of timing in programme execution. **9** Remember that each BITSER programme has a different effect; don't treat them the same. **10** Don't expect immediate expertise; practical experience is essential.

This list summarises the core principles and recommendations from chapter 5, aimed at effective implementation of the BITSER method.

ISN'T IT GREAT WHEN YOU ALWAYS KNOW IN ADVANCE

THAT YOU WILL ACHIEVE YOUR GOALS?

PREDICT YOUR RESULTS BEFORE ROLLING OUT YOUR PROGRAMMES

Imagine always knowing in advance that you'll achieve your goals. Sounds like a dream come true, doesn't it? In the business world, this dream is closer to reality than you might think, thanks to the BITSER method.

Let's start with a simple analogy that illustrates the essence of result prediction:

The Restaurant vs. The Casino

When you go out for dinner, you order without a strict budget limit. And you know what you're getting for your money. In a casino, however, most people set a strict limit. Why this difference? The key lies in the predictability of the outcome. This comparison teaches us two crucial lessons for business:

1	When you don't know the results of your investments, you tend to limit them.
2	When you do know the results, you invest with confidence and without unnecessary restrictions.

Organisations that impose limits on investment therefore do so because they do not know whether the investment will generate results. It is therefore significant that you know the results of your actions in advance. I'm going to teach you how to predict the results of all the activities you're going to carry out.

The BITSER Method's Predictive Model: Your Business Crystal Ball

Harness the power of foresight with the BITSER method's predictive model. This sophisticated tool acts as your business crystal ball, offering unprecedented insight into future outcomes. It builds upon the BITSER steps you've explored in previous chapters, transforming them into a dynamic forecasting system.

Key features of the predictive model:

1	Leverages data from all six BITSER steps
2	Provides accurate, actionable predictions
3	Enables proactive strategy adjustments
4	Minimises risk and maximises resource allocation

By mastering this predictive model, you'll move from reactive decision-making to proactive strategy execution, giving your business a significant competitive edge. In the world of Bitsing, guesswork is replaced by informed foresight, paving the way for enduring success: *Building a Company Built to Last*.

The BITSER model acts as a reliable predictor in the often unpredictable 'casino' of business. It tells you exactly where to place your resources for the best chance of success.

Practical applications of Bitsing predictions:

- Sales team performance
- Employee productivity
- Job application response rates
- Store visits
- Customer behaviour changes
- Increase in customer spending
- Revenue and profit growth

Activities that don't contribute to your turnover continuity goal are classified as 'hobby activities'. They're unpredictable and rarely lead to significant results. The golden rule: never take action without first knowing the results.

How it Works: The Snooker Analogy

Picture a snooker player preparing for a crucial shot. He 'practices' the motion several times, adjusting the angle and force until it feels just right. Only then does he take the actual shot. The predictive model of Bitsing does the same for your business, but based on hard facts instead of feeling. It ensures that:

1 You know exactly how to 'strike' (which actions to take)

2 You use the right 'angle and force' (optimal use of resources)

3 You achieve the desired result

By applying the predictive model, you eliminate guesswork and significantly increase your chances of success.

IF SOMEONE CLAIMS THAT NOTHING CAN BE GUARANTEED, HE JUST DOESN'T KNOW HOW TO DO IT.

Predicting in Practice: Two Essential Components

To effectively predict using the BITSER method, you need two crucial elements:

1 Percentages: your current success for each BITSER step (named 'success ratios')

2 Absolute numbers: the number of customers needed to reach your turnover goal

Let's examine these components in detail.

1

Step 1: Calculate Your Current 'Success Ratios'

The 'success ratio' indicates how effective your current activities are for each step of the BITSER process. Determine your current success percentage for each BITSER step:

BITSER step	Success ratio
B Brand awareness	
I I want you	
T Traffic	
S Sales	
E Extra sales	
R Referrals	

The Success Ratio of the B Step
What percentage of all decision-makers in your target market knows your brand or organisation's name? Note your answer next to step B (Brand awareness).

The Success Ratio of the I Step
The next question relates to those standing on the B step. What percentage of those who know your name are considering your brand, want it, and put it on their list of options? Note your answer next to step I (I want you).

The Success Ratio of the T Step
The next question relates to those standing on the T step. What percentage of the considerers takes action - for example visits the store or attends a meeting? Note the answer next to the T step (Traffic).

The Success Ratio of the S Step
What percentage of the previous step's action-takers proceed to actually purchase, become a customer? Note your answer next to step S (Sales).

The Success Ratio of the E Step
What percentage of the people who have bought once remain customers and buy again? Note your answer next to the E step (Extra sales). This is called the retention percentage.

The Success Ratio of the R Step
What percentage of these returning customers actively recruits new customers when requested? Note your answer next to the R step (Referrals).

The success percentages give you a clear picture of where your organisation currently stands and where the greatest opportunities for improvement lie. When in doubt about a percentage research it among the target group. Nine out of ten organisations already have the information they need - perhaps concealed somewhere in a department. In any event - the needed information is to be found.

What Did You Learn from the Success Ratios?

The percentages indicate the current situation on each of the BITSER steps: how well the current activities of the organisation perform, measured in terms of results. The success ratios reveal:

1 Current performance:
these percentages provide a snapshot of your organisation's effectiveness at each BITSER step, quantifying how well your current activities translate into tangible results.

But they also tell you something extremely unusual. Something with significant positive impact on your turnover goal.

2 Hidden opportunities: more importantly, these ratios unlock a powerful insight into your business's untapped potential.

Calculating Turnover Potential

The success ratios enable you to calculate the total turnover 'potential' of a target group, as a result of your current activities. Here's how:

1 Select a sample: choose 100 decision-makers from your target group.

2 Sequentially apply your success ratios to this sample.

3 Predict outcomes: the result forecasts what you can expect from your current sales activities.

You will then have predicted what you can expect from your current sales activities. Let's illustrate with an example (read from top to bottom):

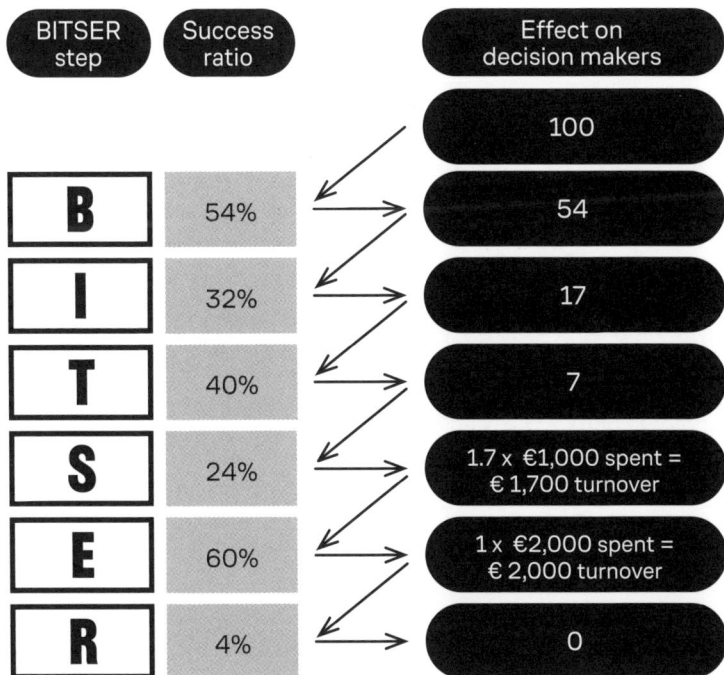

BITSER step	Success ratio	Effect on decision makers
		100
B	54%	54
I	32%	17
T	40%	7
S	24%	1.7 x €1,000 spent = € 1,700 turnover
E	60%	1 x €2,000 spent = € 2,000 turnover
R	4%	0

This predictive model offers a clear view of your current effectiveness and, more crucially, highlights areas for improvement. By optimising these ratios, you can dramatically increase your turnover without necessarily expanding your target audience.

The Power of Optimisation: A Practical Example

Now let's see how this information helps you predict and optimise your results. We'll use the previously mentioned success ratios and a hypothetical group of 100 potential decision-makers in your target market.

Out of 100 decision-makers:

1	54% know your brand (B: 54 people)
2	32% of them consider your brand (I: 17 people)
3	40% take action (T: 7 people)
4	24% actually buy (S: 2 people)
5	60% remain a customer and buy again (E: 1 person)
6	4% recruit new customers (R: 0.04 people, or 1 in 25 customers)

Assuming each buyer spends an average of €1,850 this results in revenue of €3,700 per 100 decision-makers approached.

And here comes the magic of the Bitsing predictive model: What happens if we optimise these percentages? Suppose that targeted BITSER programmes can increase the I-step success ratio from 32% to 49%. Let's calculate the effect:

Out of 100 decision-makers:

- 54% still know your brand (B: 54 people)
- Now 49% consider your brand (I: 26 people, was 17)
- 40% take action (T: 10 people, was 7)
- 24% actually buy (S: 3 people, was 2)

This optimisation of the I-step alone increases your revenue from €3,700 to €5,550 per 100 decision-makers – a growth of 50%! In the BITSER method, success ratios are not just metrics – they're your roadmap to unlocking exponential growth.

2

Step 2: Calculate the Required Number of Customers

Now that you know how effective your current activities are, the next step is to determine how many customers you need to reach your revenue goal. The actual, required number of customers is easily calculated. Three elements are required: your turnover target, the average amount spent by a typical customer, and a formula – this simple but powerful formula:

Required number of customers = turnover goal divided by average annual spend per typical customer

Let's apply this in a practical example:

Suppose your turnover goal is €1,000,000 for the coming year. You've calculated that a typical customer spends, on average, €100 per year on your products or services.

Required number of customers = 1,000,000 / 100 = 10,000 customers. This means you need 10,000 active customers to reach your turnover goal.

An Important tip: The average amount spent can fluctuate due to various factors such as seasonal influences, economic conditions or changes in your product offering. Check this number regularly and adjust your calculation if necessary.

Creating a BITSER Results Prediction: A Step-by-Step Guide

You've now successfully predicted the number of customers required to achieve your turnover goal. This crucial piece of information serves as the foundation for the next phase of your Result prediction. Don't be intimidated – this process is straightforward and logical.

1

Begin with the SER Steps

The total number of required customers comprises two categories:

a)   Existing customers to retain (E step)
b)   New clients to acquire (S and R steps)

An example of an SER results prediction:

	Number	Succes ratio	Prediction
S			213
E	300	60%	180
R	180	4%	7

Calculation process:

1   E Step: apply the success ratio to your current customer base. Example: 300 existing customers × 60% retention rate = 180 retained customers predicted!

2   R Step: calculate new customers from referrals. Example: 180 retained customers × 4% referral rate = 7 new customers acquired via existing customers.

3   S Step: determine remaining customers needed. Example: If 400 total customers are required to achieve the turnover goal, S step = 400 - (180 + 7) = 213 new customers to recruit.

2

Continue with the BIT Steps

Use the S step result to predict outcomes for the BIT programmes. Example calculation for T step:

4	S step result: 213 new customers to recruit
5	S step success ratio: 24%
6	T step calculation: 100/24 × 213 = 887

Repeat this process for the B and I steps. A schematic example of a BIT results prediction:

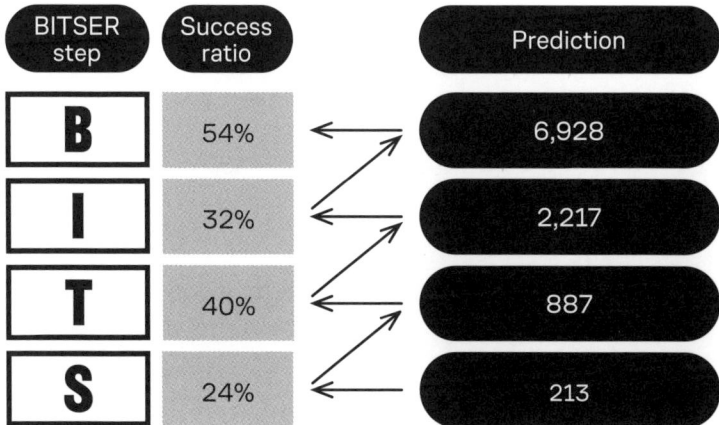

BITSER step	Success ratio		Prediction
B	54%	←	6,928
I	32%	←	2,217
T	40%	←	887
S	24%	←	213

3

From Prediction to Target Group Reach

The 'required programme reach' is crucial for each BITSER step. It represents the number of people each programme must approach to achieve the predicted outcome.

	Reach		Succes ratio		Result prediction
B	12,829	←	54%	←	6,928
I	6,928	←	32%	←	2,217
T	2,217	←	40%	←	887
S	887	←	24%	←	213

Note: the number of people to be approached via the E programme is a special case. The people to be reached on the E step are all existing customers.

E	300	←	60%	←	180
R	180	←	4%	←	7

Note: The E programme reach is unique, targeting all existing customers.

About Reach

Reach refers to the number of target group individuals to be approached with a BITSER programme. In this example, to achieve your turnover goal and build a healthy company that lasts, you need to reach the following numbers of people:

12,829 individuals with the B programme

6,928 individuals (Potentials) with the I programme

2,217 individuals (Preferrers) with the T programme

887 individuals (Movers) with the S programme

300 Buyers with the E programme

180 Users with the R programme

Now create a reach prediction for your own goal.

Handling Insufficient Target Group Size

This applies if your required reach exceeds your available target group. For example, what if there aren't 12,829 individuals (Suspects) available in our target group? What if the target group is too small?

1	Compare total available targets (excluding current customers) with the number reached on the B step.
2	If there's a shortfall, focus on improving the lowest-performing BITSER step ratios.
3	Optimise these ratios until the B programme reach aligns with your available target group.

Example   A railway company's turnover target

I once worked with a railway company that needed to reach 60 million consumers to hit its turnover target. The problem? Only 33 million were available. You can't achieve goals with non-existent customers, no matter how hard you try. Yet, surprisingly, the company succeeded! How? By optimising poor success ratios.

Checking and Updating Your BITSER Ranking

Use success ratios to verify your BITSER ranking. Lower ratios should correspond to higher priority rankings. Compare the two rankings alongside the success ratios. Which of the two is correct?

	Succes Ratio	Ranking 1	Ranking 2
B	54%	5	4
I	32%	1	3
T	40%	4	6
S	24%	2	1
E	60%	6	5
R	4%	3	2

A Crucial Tip!

The lower a success ratio, the higher the relevant BITSER step will rank. Starting at the beginning of the BITSER stairway, lower success ratios must receive higher priority in terms of ranking.

So, always work from top to bottom. The B step at the top always involves the most people, while the R step at the bottom involves the fewest. Even if the B ratio is 20% and the R ratio is slightly lower at 15%, B should still receive a higher rank. Why? Because improving the B ratio affects more people; thus has a greater impact on achieving your turnover goal.

In developing BITSER ranking, volume matters as much as percentages. A small improvement at the top can cascade into significant gains throughout the process.

What if the Facts Change?

As success ratios change, update your predictions. Higher ratios mean fewer people to reach, improving cost efficiency. Lower ratios may require reaching more people.

Results Prediction: A Blueprint for Organisational Structure

The predictive model's power lies in its adaptability and data-driven approach. Regularly update your predictions to stay aligned with current realities and to optimise your business strategy.

Predicting results through the BITSER method is not just about forecasting; it's a fundamental tool for shaping your entire organisation. Here's how:

1 — **Comprehensive preparation:**

Knowing the reach and expected results of each BITSER programme allows you to prepare your organisation effectively for future challenges.

This foresight impacts everything from resource allocation to team structures.

2 — **Inclusive goal setting:**

Involve all stakeholders in the prediction process - from you and your colleagues to all relevant parties.

Clear communication of goals is crucial; people can't achieve targets they don't know about.

3 **Detailed operational insights:**

Predictions provide specific metrics:
number of people to approach, expected visitors
and projected customer conversions.

These insights directly influence organisational
structure and resource deployment.

4 **Department-specific benefits:**

Marketing: gains clear requirements
for support and media planning.

Sales: understands target reactions,
numbers to be approached and expected results.

After-sales: knows how many existing customers
to engage for additional sales.

5 **Organisation-wide alignment:**

Every employee understands their role
in achieving the predicted results.

This alignment ensures a cohesive approach
to meeting organisational goals.

6 **Dynamic structuring:**

As predictions change, your organisational
structure can adapt accordingly.

This flexibility allows for responsive,
efficient operations.

By integrating the BITSER predictions into your organisational planning, you create a data-driven, goal-oriented structure that is primed for success. This approach ensures that every part of your organisation is not just aware of its targets, but is optimally positioned to achieve them.

Key Learnings for Effective Prediction

1 Know your numbers: regularly update your success ratios for each BITSER step.

2 Understand your customer value: keep track of the average amount spent by the typical customer.

3 Set clear goals: have a defined turnover target for the period you're predicting.

4 Use the formula: consistently apply the customer calculation formula to stay on track.

5 Optimise strategically: focus on improving those BITSER steps with the lowest percentages, for maximum impact.

Avoiding Common Pitfalls

1 Don't assume: always base your predictions on actual data, not wishful thinking.

2 Stay flexible: be prepared to adjust your strategies if your Bitsing prediction indicates suboptimal results.

3 Look beyond sales: remember that improvements in awareness (B) and interest (I) can have significant downstream effects.

4 Don't neglect any step: each BITSER step is crucial; ignoring one can create a bottleneck in your success pipeline.

Implementing BITSER Predictions in Your Organisation

1 Educate your team: ensure everyone understands the BITSER steps and their importance.

2 Collect data regularly: set up systems to continuously gather data for each BITSER step.

3 Create a prediction routine: make result prediction a regular part of your planning process.

4 Act on insights: use the predictions to guide your strategy and resource allocation.

5 Monitor and adjust: regularly compare actual results with predictions and refine your approach.

The Power of Predictable Success

By mastering the art of results prediction with the predictive model of Bitsing, you transform your business approach from hopeful guesswork to strategic certainty. This not only boosts your confidence, it also allows for more efficient use of resources, targeted improvements and, ultimately, the achievement of your revenue goals.

Remember, in the world of Bitsing you're not just playing the game – you're changing the odds in your favour. With each prediction and subsequent optimisation, you're building a more resilient, successful and profitable business. In the next section, we'll delve deeper into how to use these predictions to fine-tune your BITSER programmes and create a roadmap.

Creating a BITSER Programme Calendar

Develop a calendar for each sub-period, that includes:

1	Turnover targets
2	Required programme reach
3	Predicted results

Regularly update this calendar based on actual results and changing circumstances. Remember to account for the time lag between initiating programmes and achieving turnover. You'll often be implementing current programmes while preparing for future periods. By following these steps and continuously refining your approach, you'll create a robust, data-driven strategy for achieving your turnover goals using the Bitsing method.

The following learnings emphasise the systematic, data-driven approach of the BITSER method in achieving business goals through accurate prediction and strategic planning.

1

Predictive power: The BITSER method allows you to predict results accurately before implementing programmes, enabling proactive strategy development.

2

Structured approach:
Always start with the SER (Sales, Extra Sales, Referrals) steps before moving to the BIT (Brand awareness, Interest, Traffic) steps when making predictions.

3

Success ratio importance: Success ratios are crucial in calculating the required number of customers for each BITSER step and in prioritising improvement efforts.

4

Top-down priority: Improvements in higher steps (like Brand awareness) often have a more significant impact due to the larger number of people affected.

5

Target group sizing: The method can identify if your target group is too small to achieve your goals, allowing for timely strategy adjustments.

6

Optimisation techniques:
In the case of an undersized target group, focus on improving the success ratios of the most critical steps rather than trying to expand the target group.

7 **Dynamic adaptation:** Regularly update predictions as circumstances change, ensuring your strategy remains relevant and effective.

8 **Organisational alignment:** Use BITSER predictions to structure your organisation, aligning all departments towards common, quantifiable goals.

9 **Cost efficiency:** Improving success ratios can lead to reaching fewer people in order to get the same results, potentially reducing costs.

10 **Departmental integration:** Every department (marketing, sales, after-sales) can benefit from clear, quantifiable targets derived from BITSER predictions.

11 **Continuous Improvement:** The method encourages ongoing optimisation of processes and strategies based on real-time data and predictions.

THE LEARNINGS FROM THIS CHAPTER

The Do's

1 Always start with predicting the results of the SER steps (Sales, Extra Sales, Referrals) before moving to the BIT steps. **2** Use the success ratios to calculate the required number of customers for each BITSER step. **3** Work from top to bottom when prioritising improvements, as changes at the top (B step) affect more people and have a greater impact. **4** Regularly update your predictions as facts and circumstances change. **5** Involve all stakeholders in the prediction process and communicate goals clearly. **6** Use the BITSER predictions to structure your organisation and align all departments. **7** Create a BITSER programme calendar for each sub-period to track and adjust your strategies. **8** Optimise your success ratios if you face a 'red flag' situation where your target group is too small.

The Don'ts

1 Don't ignore the importance of the 'required programme reach' for each BITSER step. **2** Don't assume that a higher success ratio always means higher priority; consider the volume of people affected. **3** Don't neglect to adjust your strategy if the available target group is smaller than required. **4** Don't keep your predictions to yourself; share them with all relevant parties in your organisation. **5** Don't stick rigidly to initial predictions; be prepared to adapt as circumstances change. **6** Don't focus solely on percentages; remember that absolute numbers are equally important in the BITSER method. **7** Don't try to implement all BITSER programmes at once if facing a red flag situation; focus on optimising the problematic ratios first. **8** Don't underestimate the impact of external factors (like weather) on your success ratios; always be ready to recalculate. **9** Don't assume that improving all ratios equally is the best approach; prioritise based on the BITSER ranking. **10** Don't forget to consider the time lag between implementing programmes and achieving turnover when creating your BITSER calendar.

KEY TRAPS TO AVOID

By being aware of these pitfalls you can navigate implementation more effectively, ensuring a more successful application of the strategy.

1 **Ignoring the hierarchy:** Failing to work from top to bottom in the BITSER steps; potentially missing the most impactful improvements.

2 **Overemphasising percentages:** Focusing solely on success ratios without considering the absolute number of people affected at each step.

3 **Target group misjudgement:** Not recognising when your target group is too small to achieve your goals, leading to unrealistic expectations.

4 **Inflexibility:** Sticking rigidly to initial predictions without adapting to changing circumstances or new data.

5 **Siloed thinking:** Keeping predictions within a small team instead of sharing them across the organisation, hindering alignment and buy-in.

6 **Neglecting the calendar:** Failing to create or update a BITSER programme calendar, leading to poor timing in programme implementation.

7 **Blanket optimisation:** Trying to improve all BITSER steps equally instead of prioritising based on the BITSER ranking and potential impact.

8 **Overlooking external factors:** Not considering how external elements (like economic changes or weather) might affect your success ratios.

9 **Short-term focus:** Neglecting to account for the time lag between programme implementation and actual results in turnover.

10 **Misallocating resources:** Investing in all six BITSER programmes simultaneously when facing a 'red flag' situation, instead of focusing on optimising critical ratios first.

11 **Assumption of stability:** Believing that once calculated, success ratios will remain constant without need for regular reassessment.

12 **Neglecting organisational structure:** Failing to use BITSER predictions to inform and reshape organisational structure and resource allocation.

13 **Ignoring interdependencies:** Not recognising how improvements in one BITSER step can affect others, potentially leading to missed opportunities or unexpected challenges.

14 **Over-complication:** Making the prediction process too complex, discouraging team engagement and regular updates.

15 **Undervaluing small improvements:** Dismissing small percentage improvements in higher BITSER steps, which can have significant cumulative effects.

THE GOLDEN RULE:

NEVER SPEND MORE THAN A PROGRAMME CAN EARN

ENSURING PROFIT AND AVOIDING FINANCIAL DISASTERS

Imagine paying for bread at a bakery and leaving empty-handed. Absurd, right? Yet organisations routinely invest millions in advertising without a clear idea of the return. This chapter introduces a paradigm shift in financial thinking, moving from nebulous 'investments' to strategic 'spending' with guaranteed returns.

The Pitfall of Misplaced Goals

Many organisations mistakenly elevate strategies or tasks to the status of goals, obscuring the true objective. Your continuity turnover target is the ultimate goal. Everything else is merely a means to this end. By focusing investments directly on this goal, you ensure more effective and efficient resource allocation.

An exercise: Write down your turnover goal. Now evaluate your current investments. Are they directly contributing to this goal? Would you invest a million knowing you'd only get half back? Of course not. But if you could double it? Absolutely!

Never Spend More Than Your Programmes Can Generate

During my experience in implementing the Bitsing method across various organisations I've been consistently astonished by the prevalence of haphazard budgeting. Many companies allocate funds to activities with unknown profitability, or even a potential for loss. Their justification? 'Risk is part of the cost.'

This mindset leads to blind investments and financial uncertainty. The Bitsing method fundamentally changes this approach. With the ROS model, financial allocation becomes a precise science:

1	Guaranteed Return: Money is only spent when there's certainty that the activity will generate more than it costs.
2	Profit Assurance: You don't just aim for profit; it is guaranteed.
3	Elimination of Guesswork: No more relying on gut feel or vague projections.

You might be thinking, 'Isn't this just ROI (Return on Investment)?' Not quite. In fact, I'll demonstrate why the entire concept of ROI is flawed and how the Bitsing method offers a superior alternative.

The key principles of avoiding financial disasters are:

1 All expenditure must have a clear, quantifiable return.

2 Risk is not accepted as an inevitable cost; it's minimised through strategic planning.

3 Profit is not hoped for; it's engineered into every financial decision.

By adopting this approach, organisations can transform their financial strategy from a game of chance to a precise, predictable process. The days of justifying losses as the outcome of 'necessary risks' are over. With Bitsing, every amount spent is an amount invested in guaranteed growth.

From ROI to ROS: A New Financial Paradigm

Forget Return on Investment (ROI). It's an outdated, vague concept that can mask financial disasters. ROI stands for what you get back from an investment. But what is that exactly? What do you actually get back as return on your investment? According to this definition, it could be anything. Also zero!

Enter 'Remainder on Spend' (ROS) – the Bitsing method's approach to financial success.

Why ROS trumps ROI:

1 Specificity: ROS focuses on the actual money left after spending, not just on 'returns.'

2 Predictability: With ROS, you know the outcome before spending.

3 Profitability Focus: ROS ensures you always end up with more than you spend.

Preventing Financial Disasters

The key to financial success is knowing in advance whether an activity will deliver ROS. Post-evaluation is too late. Here's how to ensure your BITSER programmes always bring in more than they cost:

1 Quantify expected returns: Before any spend, calculate the precise expected return.

2 Compare spend to return: Ensure the return always exceeds the spend.

3 Focus on turnover goal: Every spend should directly contribute to your continuity turnover target.

4 Avoid haphazard budgeting: Never allocate funds without a clear, quantifiable return expectation.

5 Think 'spend,' not 'Invest': Investments imply uncertainty; spending implies known returns.

Implementing ROS in Your Organisation

1 Analyse current spending: review all current 'investments'. Are they yielding positive ROS?

2 Develop ROS forecasts: for every proposed programme or activity, create a detailed ROS forecast.

3 Set ROS thresholds: establish minimum ROS requirements for programme approval.

4 Regular ROS reviews: continuously monitor actual ROS against forecasts, adjusting strategies as needed.

5 Educate your team: ensure everyone understands and applies the ROS concept in their decision-making.

Example — The bakery principle

Consider a bakery investing in a new oven. Traditional ROI might focus on increased production capacity. ROS asks:

- Exact cost of the oven?
- Precise increase in daily bread production?
- Additional revenue from increased production?
- Maintenance and operation costs?

The bakery should only proceed if the remainder (additional revenue minus all costs) is positive.

The Power of ROS

By adopting the ROS mindset, you transform your organisation's financial approach. Every spend becomes a strategic move towards your turnover goal, eliminating wasteful 'investments' and ensuring consistent profitability. In the world of Bitsing, we don't invest hoping for returns; we spend knowing we'll have a remainder. This shift in thinking is your key to avoiding financial disasters and building a sustainably profitable organisation.

IT'S NOT ABOUT ROI
(RETURN ON INVESTMENT)
BUT ABOUT ROS
(REMAINDER ON SPEND).

Transforming Financial Planning with ROS

The Bitsing method introduces a revolutionary approach to financial planning: predicting and guaranteeing Remainder on Spend (ROS). This section outlines the practical steps to implement this powerful concept, ensuring your organisation always spends less than it earns.

Four-step ROS analysis:

❶	Calculate profit
❷	Determine BITSER expenditure ceiling
❸	Quantify BITSER expenditure plan
❹	Predict yield (ROS)

1

Step 1: Calculate Profit

Profit is the positive difference between turnover and total costs. In our example, a company with a €175,000,000 turnover goal aims for a €17,500,000 profit (10%). If profit isn't your objective, use the amount that covers expenditure.

2

Step 2: Determine BITSER Expenditure Ceiling

The Expenditure Ceiling is the maximum amount that can be spent on a programme without incurring a loss. It equals your profit target. Allocate this ceiling across BITSER programmes using strategy focus percentages:

	Strategy*	Ceiling*
B	15%	€ 2,500,000
I	30%	€ 5,000,000
T	20%	€ 3,300,000
S	25%	€ 4,150,000
E	10%	€ 1,700,000
R	5%	€ 850,000
	105%	€ 17,500,000

*The focus percentages are rounded (See chapter 5). The total of all the percentages is 105%. The amounts under 'ceiling' are based on unrounded percentages.

3

Step 3: Quantify the BITSER Expenditure Plan

Detail the actual costs for developing and implementing each BITSER programme. Include direct programme costs and relevant personnel expenses. Ensure expenditures align with programme strategy percentages.

4

Step 4: Predict Remainder on Spend (ROS)

ROS is the difference between the Expenditure Ceiling and the Expenditure Plan. A positive ROS indicates profitable spending.

	Strategy*	Ceiling*	Expenditure	ROS
B	15%	€ 2,500,000	€ 290,000	€ 2,210,000
I	30%	€ 5,000,000	€ 580,000	€ 4,420,000
T	20%	€ 3,300,000	€ 385,000	€ 2,915,000
S	25%	€ 4,150,000	€ 490,000	€ 3,660,000
E	10%	€ 1,700,000	€ 170,000	€ 1,530,000
R	5%	€ 850,000	€ 85,000	€ 765,000
	105%	€ 17,500,000	€ 2,000,000	€ 15,500,000

Handling Unexpected Expenditures

Monitor actual expenditures against ROS and the ceiling. Additional costs that fall within a positive ROS won't impact profit. Exceeding the ceiling leads to losses. Use these benchmarks to make quick decisions on unforeseen expenses.

BITSER Programme Share of Turnover

Each BITSER programme contributes to overall turnover. Omitting a programme risks losing substantial revenue. Example for a €250,000,000 turnover goal:

	Focus strategy*	Share of turnover
B	20%	€ 50,000,000
I	30%	€ 75,000,000
T	25%	€ 62,500,000
S	10%	€ 25,000,000
E	5%	€ 12,500,000
R	15%	€ 37,500,000

*Total turnover exceeds turnover goal by 5% due to rounding.

Note: Scrapping the I programme risks losing €75,000,000 in turnover. Focusing solely on sales (S programme) would only guarantee €25,000,000, just 17% of the goal.

The Power of ROS in Practice

The ROS model, while simplified here, has been successfully applied in complex business environments. Hewlett Packard Enterprise EMEA, for instance, implemented this across all data streams, resulting in nearly tripled turnover. By adopting the ROS approach, organisations can:

1	Ensure every programme contributes positively to the bottom line
2	Make informed decisions about resource allocation
3	Quickly identify and address potential financial risks
4	Maintain a clear focus on the overall turnover goal
5	Adapt swiftly to unexpected financial challenges

In the world of Bitsing, it's not about return on investment (ROI), but about remainder on spend (ROS). This shift in perspective guarantees that every euro spent contributes directly to your financial success.

These key learnings emphasise the core of the Bitsing method: a data-driven, predictable approach to financial management that aims for guaranteed profitability. By adopting these principles, organisations can transform their financial strategy from a game of chance to a precise, controllable process.

1	Focus on ROS (Remainder on Spend) instead of ROI: ROS provides a more precise and reliable measure of financial success.
2	Never spend more than a programme can generate: Every expenditure must have a guaranteed positive return.
3	Centre all investments around the turnover goal: All spending should directly contribute to achieving the continuity turnover target.
4	Utilise the BITSER expenditure ceiling method: This helps determine the maximum spend per programme without incurring losses.
5	Implement a detailed BITSER expenditure plan: This ensures accurate allocation of resources to each programme.
6	Predict and guarantee yield (ROS) for each programme: Ensure expenditures always remain below the ceiling for a positive ROS.
7	Understand each BITSER programme's contribution to total turnover: This aids in making informed decisions about resource allocation.

8	Be cautious with unexpected expenditures: Monitor these carefully against ROS and the expenditure ceiling.
9	Avoid haphazard budgeting: Base all financial decisions on concrete, predictable outcomes.
10	Adapt an organisational structure based on ROS predictions: This ensures more efficient and effective business operations.
11	Involve all stakeholders in the ROS process: This ensures organisation-wide alignment on financial goals.
12	Be flexible and adjust strategies based on ROS results: Continuous monitoring and adaptation are essential for success.

CRITICAL PITFALLS TO BE AWARE OF

By being aware of these pitfalls, organisations can more effectively implement the Bitsing method, ensuring a more predictable and profitable financial strategy.

1 **Relying on traditional ROI:**
Mistaking ROI for a reliable measure of financial success, when it can mask potential losses.

2 **Haphazard budgeting:**
Allocating funds to activities without a clear understanding of their profitability potential.

3 **Risk acceptance mentality:**
Justifying potential losses as an inevitable part of business, rather than seeking to minimise or eliminate them.

4 **Overlooking programme interdependencies:**
Failing to recognise how each BITSER programme contributes to overall turnover, which will potentially lead to underinvestment in crucial areas.

5 **Exceeding expenditure ceilings:**
Spending more on a programme than its designated ceiling, risking profitability.

6 **Neglecting unexpected costs:**
Failing to account for and properly manage unforeseen expenses within the ROS framework.

7 **Misalignment with turnover goals:**
Investing in activities that don't directly
contribute to the continuity turnover target.

8 **Inflexibility in spending:**
Sticking rigidly to initial plans when
ROS predictions suggest a need for adjustment.

9 **Siloed financial planning:**
Not involving all stakeholders in the ROS process,
leading to misaligned expectations and efforts.

10 **Overemphasis on sales:**
Focusing solely on the S (Sales) programme while
neglecting other crucial BITSER components.

11 **Ignoring the expenditure plan:**
Failing to create or adhere to a detailed BITSER
expenditure plan aligned with programme strategies.

12 **Misunderstanding programme contributions:**
Assuming all BITSER programmes contribute equally
to turnover, leading to misallocation of resources.

13 **Short-term thinking:**
Prioritising immediate returns over long-term
financial health and sustainable growth.

14 **Lack of continuous monitoring:**
Failing to regularly track actual expenditures against
ROS predictions and expenditure ceilings.

15 **Resistance to organisational change:**
Not adapting the company structure to align
with ROS predictions and requirements.

THE LEARNINGS FROM THIS CHAPTER

The Do's

1 Do focus on Remainder on Spend (ROS) instead of Return on Investment (ROI). **2** Do calculate profit and set clear financial goals before planning expenditures. **3** Do determine the BITSER Expenditure Ceiling for each programme. **4** Do create a detailed BITSER Expenditure Plan aligned with programme strategies. **5** Do predict and guarantee a positive ROS for each BITSER programme. **6** Do monitor actual expenditures against ROS and the expenditure ceiling, regularly. **7** Do involve all stakeholders in the ROS prediction and planning process. **8** Do adapt your organisational structure based on ROS predictions. **9** Do understand and consider each BITSER programme's contribution to total turnover. **10** Do be flexible and adjust strategies based on ROS results.

THE LEARNINGS FROM THIS CHAPTER

The Don'ts

1 Don't invest more money than your programmes can generate. **2** Don't make budgets available for activities with unknown profitability or loss potential. **3** Don't justify losses or risky spending with 'risk is part of the cost' mentality. **4** Don't rely on traditional ROI calculations for financial decision-making. **5** Don't exceed the expenditure ceiling for any BITSER programme. **6** Don't neglect unexpected expenditures; always evaluate them against ROS and ceilings. **7** Don't focus solely on sales (S programme) while neglecting other BITSER components. **8** Don't implement BITSER programmes without first predicting their financial impact. **9** Don't assume all BITSER programmes contribute equally to turnover. **10** Don't stick rigidly to initial plans if ROS predictions indicate a need for change.

By following these do's and avoiding the don'ts, organisations can effectively implement the Bitsing method's financial approach, ensuring more predictable and profitable outcomes.

Glossary

BITS

To bits an organisation's plans or decisions is to test or evaluate them using the Bitsing method. To bits is to check and optimize existing and planned activities. 'We have to bits this programme' means that the programme has to be made to conform to the Bitsing criteria.

BITSED

A process is or has been bitsed once it has successfully fulfilled the requirements of the Bitsing method and has been evaluated and optimised. 'The programme is bitsed' means it has been tested against and complies with the Bitsing requirements.

BITSER

The person within an organisation responsible for bitsing. A bitser has acquired knowledge through training courses, seminars or other sources. A bitser understands the methodology, but is not yet an expert in the field (See 'Bitseter').

BITSETER

A person trained in the art of Bitsing.
A Bitseter can professionally apply
the methodology and generate Bitsing
plans and advice. A Bitseter often has
a recognised tertiary degree which
includes a Bitsing component.

BITSING

Bitsing is the entire discipline. The field
or world of Bitsing. Also indicated by the
umbrella term, 'Bitsing method', as used in
this book. Organisations in the process of
actively applying the Bitsing method in
their operations are 'bitsing'.

BITSING METHOD

The Bitsing method comprises three
elements: the seven laws or principles
to be followed, the models you use and
a range of analysis criteria which give
substance to Bitsing plans. has to be made
to conform to the Bitsing criteria.

Bitsing, Bitsing method, Bitser, Bitseter,
Bits, Bitsed... are terms you will increasingly
frequently encounter.

The Bitsing Method
Seven Principles for Building Companies to Last

The Bitsing method represents a ground-breaking approach to business strategy and operational and financial management, promising guaranteed results. Developed through years of practical experience and refined through numerous case studies, this method consists of seven fundamental principles, each building upon the previous one to create a comprehensive framework for business success.

1

At the heart of the Bitsing method lies the concept of the continuity turnover goal. This is not just any financial target, it's the amount of turnover your business needs to sustain itself and thrive in the long term. This goal must be specific, quantifiable, and focused on long-term sustainability rather than short-term gains. It requires a holistic approach, considering all aspects of your business when setting this goal. This foundational principle serves as the basis for all subsequent strategies and actions in the Bitsing method.

2

This principle emphasizes the importance of identifying your money sources, based on hard financial facts. Success in business depends on understanding where your revenue comes from and targeting those who contribute most significantly to your continuity turnover goal. This involves gaining detailed insights into your money sources, analyzing the growth potential and value of different segments, and focusing your efforts on the most valuable ones. By aligning all activities—such as marketing and sales efforts—towards these ideal money sources, your business will maximize its efficiency and effectiveness.

3

The third principle of the Bitsing method focuses on identifying and leveraging your company's uncopyable advantage - what we call 'The Golden Egg'. This is the factor that sets your business apart from competitors and makes you truly unbeatable in the market.

4

The fourth principle introduces the BITSER model to map this journey. BITSER stands for Brand Awareness, Interest, Traffic, Sales, Extra Sales, and Referrals. This comprehensive view considers all stages of customer interaction, ensuring that each step can be quantified and analysed. By mapping out each stage of the customer's journey using the BITSER model, businesses can identify key touchpoints and interactions, develop strategies to optimise each step, and regularly measure and analyse performance at each stage. This fourth principle recognises that not all aspects of the customer journey are equally important or effective. The Bitsing method introduces a ranking system to prioritise efforts and resources. This efficiency-focused approach uses data-driven decision making to concentrate on the most impactful activities. It also emphasises the need for flexibility, encouraging businesses to shift priorities, based on performance data. By analysing the performance of each BITSER stage and identifying areas with the lowest performance or highest potential for improvement, businesses can allocate resources and efforts more effectively.

5

With priorities set, the fifth principle focuses on developing specific programmes for each stage of the BITSER model. These programmes should be tailored to move customers effectively through their journey. Each programme must be customised for its specific BITSER stage, goal-oriented to directly contribute to the continuity turnover goal, and include clear, measurable KPIs. I named them BPIs – Bitsing Performance Insights. This fifth principle ensures that all business activities are strategically aligned and measurable.

6

One of the most powerful aspects of the Bitsing method is its emphasis on predicting results before investing resources. The sixth principle introduces this predictive approach, which minimises risk and maximises efficiency. By mastering the art of result prediction, businesses can transform their approach from reactive to proactive, setting the stage for sustainable growth and long-term success. This predictive capability is a key factor in building companies that are not just successful today, but are truly built to last.

7

The final principle focuses on financial management, introducing the concept of Remainder on Spend (ROS) as a replacement for traditional Return on Investment (ROI). This principle ensures that every expenditure generates more than it costs by setting clear expenditure ceilings for each programme and using ROS predictions to guide all financial decisions.

Important Tip!

While each principle is powerful on its own, the true strength of the Bitsing method lies in their *integration*.

BITSING CHECKLIST SUMMARY

1 Have you determined your revenue goal?

2 Have you identified the revenue sources, their share in the revenue, and determined the focus growth strategy?

3 And derived from that, the non-copyable emotional brand positioning themes, rational product sales themes, and relational organizational loyalty themes, communication themes?

4 Do you know what your organization's golden egg is, and from that, the non-copyable emotional, rational, and relational (brand preference, product buying and organization loyalty themes) positioning/communication themes?

5 Has the BITSER activity prioritization plan been developed?

6 When implementing the program activities, are you considering primary effectiveness techniques?

7 Have the results of the planned activity programs been predicted?

8 Do you have the ROS in sight, ensuring that less money will be spent on program activities than they will generate, thus guaranteeing a positive return?

Measurement is Knowledge
Foresight is the Essence of Governance

Measurement is vital! I'm tempted to say that measurement is the most crucial aspect of the Bitsing method, were it not for the fact that all other aspects are equally important. It is, however, absolutely essential. Without measurement, you can't operate on the basis of facts - and factual information is the backbone of this methodology.

Circumstances change - and so do the answers provided by the Bitsing method. I believe in enjoying life, but in a way that allows me to live as long as possible - otherwise, there won't be time to do all that I still want to do. It's about balancing pleasure and health, you might say. There are times when it's hard to find that balance, when pleasure takes the upper hand. And there are times I stand on the scale – which never fails to tell me when it's time for a little lifestyle adjustment. So I adjust. I exercise more, eat healthier, get more sleep.

Organisations, too, have lives. They should also do every-thing they can to live as long as possible, without denying themselves some pleasure. An organisation will therefore also have to regularly bring itself back into balance, to remain healthy and keep its employees happy.

We weigh ourselves, so why don't organisations check how they measure up? If you don't know something is wrong, you can do nothing to fix it. Ignorance is far from bliss. So measure!

Evaluating your programmes' results equips you to enter the next phase. However, the aspects that affect your choices change. All the issues I described in the seven laws will change over time. Which means you have to change your reaction to them by updating your Bitsing plan. This is the only way you can ensure that future turnover targets will continue to be achieved, with yield.

What would happen if a new product or service becomes dominant in terms of its share of your turnover? It will have to become the new topic in your purchasing behaviour programmes. What if the average customer order amount changes? It will influence the number of customers you need to recruit and retain, and therefore the prediction of your programmes' results. In short, monitoring, measurement, evaluation, learning from experience and adapting are all essential for the healthy survival of your organisation.

Investigate whether the facts on which your Bitsing plan is based have changed, draw lessons from this, and make the necessary adjustments. The contents of this book are your best guide to what has to be measured and how.

Closing Remarks

As you reach the end of this book, I hope you're as inspired as I am by the power and potential of the Bitsing method. As someone who's always seeking ways to improve processes and optimise results, I'm convinced that Bitsing is an invaluable tool for any entrepreneur or anybody striving for measurable growth and success.

I challenge you to apply the principles we've discussed in your own context. Experiment with them, adapt them where necessary, and observe the results. Don't be afraid to fail; every failure is an opportunity to learn and refine your approach. And finally: base your decisions and actions as much as possible on facts. Be assured, everything you do will succeed. The wish is not father to the thought - facts are!

I encourage you to share your experiences. As a community of professionals, we can learn from and inspire each other. Your successes and challenges can provide valuable insights for others walking the same path. Please also go to bitsing.com/growth and answer a brief question. Your answer will show that something unexpected has happened to you. And do it today, because you have a lot of 'bitsness' coming up.

I'll leave you with a kind of wish... That you will achieve all the results you strive for and enjoy them to the fullest. This is why you are on earth: to fully enjoy the positive things in life.

Since discovering the Bitsing method, I have come to realise that anything is possible. I hope I have instilled this belief in you. If so, I have achieved my goal. With entrepreneurial regards and perhaps till we meet again,

Frans de Groot

A Thank You

Following my discovery of Bitsing, I had the privilege of coaching and inspiring countless businesses, institutions and organisations (and thousands of individuals) with this method. For decades, in locations across the globe, I have taken people on a journey into the world of Bitsing, enabling them to effortlessly achieve their most ambitious goals.

And succeed they did! Over the years, numerous positive messages and success stories have resulted. Some of these stories are too remarkable not to include in this book. Out of respect for privacy, I have limited myself to mentioning the organisations the individuals represent, and not used their own names. Nevertheless, I want to extend a special thank-you to those who took the time and made the effort to share their experiences and successes with me.

Thank you all – as well as everyone who has embraced Bitsing. I'm proud of you!